Pastors under pressure

Conflicts on the outside, conflicts within

James Taylor

DayOne

© Day One Publications 2001
First printed 2001

Scripture quotations are from The New International Version.
© 1982 Thomas Nelson Inc.

British Library Cataloguing in Publication Data available
ISBN 1 903087 10 4

Published by Day One Publications
3 Epsom Business Park, Kiln Lane, Epsom, Surrey KT17 1JF.
01372 728 300 **FAX** 01372 722 400
email—sales@dayone.co.uk
www.dayone.co.uk

Designed by Steve Devane and printed by Bath Press

Dedication

To my wife, Helen.

Contents

Foreword

S ince Jim Taylor and I belong to the same generation of pastors and teachers, it has been stimulating to share his identification of some of the principal pressures of present day ministry. Any period of history —and especially the last forty years—always witnessed marked changes. This has been particularly the case with regard to the ways in which people view their pastors or ministers.

The first chapter pinpoints the urgent need for pastors to identify and understand their role fully . Often congregations do not know what they require of their pastors, or their expectation of them may be different from the biblical pattern, influenced by contemporary standards and criteria. Having recently read the autobiography of one of the world's most famous football managers—Alex Ferguson—I found myself reflecting how, sadly, pastors may be treated sometimes like football managers. When the team plays well (i.e. when the congregations and the offerings grow), the members congratulate themselves upon their wisdom in choosing him. However, when the team plays badly, they want to change the manager.

The social and moral problems that contemporary pastors face are not new, but they are more numerous. Unless the spiritual tide turns, they will increase and become even more demanding upon a pastor's time and energies. However, their reality and seriousness underline the unique relevance of the gospel we hold in trust to teach and to preach.

The challenges of discouragement, criticism, loneliness, dryness, failure and temptation, that this book so honestly identifies, have always been present. Although some succumb, the majority of pastors overcome them. Through such challenges the genuineness of their call may often be confirmed. Human frailty becomes a platform on which God demonstrates that his power works best in weakness. Jim Taylor regularly and deliberately takes us to the example of our Lord Jesus Christ, and the centrality of his cross. A pastor's usefulness is directly related to his willingness to follow in his Master's footsteps.

No pastor—or prospective pastor—should be discouraged by the book's chapter titles. Neither the author nor I would have wanted to be in any other calling. To be an undershepherd of Christ's flock is the highest privilege and the most rewarding of tasks.

I am glad that the book ends with a postscript from Jim Taylor's wife.

While it is often said that when a church calls a man to be its pastor it does not also call his wife (particularly in terms of paid employment), it is also true that none can measure the importance of a wife's oneness with her husband as he exercises his calling. The Day of Judgment, and its rewards of grace, will reveal her unique importance.

Rev Derek Prime
Edinburgh

The Christian ministry, especially when it believes its origin lies in the call of God, is surely one of the greatest, if not the greatest privilege a person can enjoy in this life. To pastor a group of God's people, sharing their joys and their troubles, to study the Word of God and then open it to a congregation, especially if they are open and receptive, are experiences which are both humbling and enriching. It was no surprise, years ago, to hear that Christian ministers come high in the league table of those who find pleasure and fulfilment in their work. Many fine books have been written testifying to the joys, and presenting the challenges and responsibilities, of Christian ministry.

Yet there is a dark side. Paul experienced it. He writes of facing 'daily the pressure of my concern for all the churches' (2 Corinthians 11:28). In Macedonia his body had no rest 'but we were harassed at every turn—conflicts on the outside, fears within' (2 Corinthians 7:5). Writing to Timothy he speaks of Demas who 'has deserted me' and of Alexander who 'did me a great deal of harm' (2 Timothy 4:10,14). He calls the same Timothy, the pastor in Ephesus, to 'endure hardship with us like a good soldier of Jesus Christ' (2 Timothy 2:3). Paul is honest and open. Christian ministry is not, and never will be, easy. If you want a trouble free life, free from criticism and opposition, never encountering the signs of human fall-enness, then the Christian ministry is not for you.

Most pastors, even if they, unlike Paul, have the care of only one church, know what he was talking about. Life as a 21st century pastor, at the beginning of a new millennium, is not a soft option. Not surprisingly casu-alties abound; there is a steady fall-out rate and burn-out, often disguised by other polite names, is all too common. In pastors' conferences, when names of ill colleagues are read out for prayer, on too many occasions the illness is identified as 'exhaustion' or 'depression.'

Most pastors are accustomed to hear members of their churches, and particularly other leaders, speak of the pressures they are encountering in their secular employment. These pressures are often immense and harmful. Pastors, for that reason and others, are reluctant to speak openly of their own pressures. They are also acutely aware of the unique compensations they enjoy and experience. Yet these pressures are real and the problems they face take their toll.

At the risk of being dismissed as negative we are going to look at some of these problems and pressures. Some of them are not altogether peculiar to those who are ordained into the Christian ministry but every minister will recognise them. Every living being, for example, will be criticised from time to time, yet, along with the apostle Paul, the average pastor lives with criticism, if not as a friend, then as an uncongenial companion. Discouragement, too, is not unique to the pastor but it haunts every preacher of the Gospel who attempts to be faithful and sees little response. So we could go on.

I served as the minister of three churches over a period of forty years. They were great years in the service of good churches. Looking back there are no regrets and many satisfactions. Yet many of the problems dealt with in the following pages were encountered. The people in these churches were flawed in the sense that they still, despite claims to conversion, bore some of the signs of being descendants of Adam. I shared that with them. Certainly it is true that not all the stresses and strains of life in the pastorate are due to the other leaders or members of the church. Frequently the pastor is personally responsible for the pressures. There will be no perfect people, either pastors or their flocks, until we all reach heaven and the experiences we are going to talk about are 'done away.'

These problems were not always coped with in the most satisfactory manner and often, little help was available in print or from official sources. Experience, hard and sometimes bitter, was a good tutor. I suppose that is the reason for this book. It includes valuable lessons drawn from many sources and a fair bit of personal experience. No apology is offered for the shared personal experience. The prayer is that it may prove valuable to others called to pass the same way. What is vitally important to remember is that all that is dealt with here occurred in the context of satisfying, and generally happy, Christian ministry and for that I give God the thanks and the glory.

I am aware that I write from the perspective of a male. If as men in the Christian ministry we encounter strains and stresses, then our wives, if anything, endure more. A minister's wife was telling me something of the difficulties they were passing through. Suddenly she said, 'You know, I find my biggest problem is having to be nice to those who are giving my husband a hard time!' A colleague was somewhat shaken. He had come in from his leadership meeting where he had endured the customary monthly flak. As was his habit, he shared some of what he had endured with his wife. He was little prepared for her outburst. 'Oh, how I hate these men!' Many a husband fails to realise the unique strains and stresses experienced by his wife in these situations. She is often the only one to whom he can bare his heart and share his inmost thoughts when things are difficult. She has to watch her husband being impeded, frustrated, criticised and often she can do nothing, publicly, about it. She is all too often the only human source of his support while, in many cases, lacking adequate training and preparation for the situation she is in.

Many of us give deep and heartfelt thanks for our wives and not just for the support, understanding and help they have given. They have had their own ministry and their contribution has been immense. Certainly I feel deeply humbled by the love, companionship and ministry of Helen.

Little is said in the following pages about wives. A colleague, forced to retire early on health grounds, insisted that his wife's problems were greater than his and that I would have to say something. I agree with his assertion but I have not done as he asked. So, a book from the perspective of a wife is long overdue.

Identity

A number of us who had been involved in a caring project in the community were to be introduced to a visiting member of the Royal Family. When she learned my name and shook hands she suddenly said, 'And who are you?' Isn't it astonishing how many answers you can think of in a split second! They were all rejected equally quickly in favour of a rather limp 'I'm the local Baptist minister.' Satisfied, and showing no further interest, she passed on.

That incident raised the question of my identity as a pastor. 'Who am I?' is increasingly asked by pastors in today's culture. Like many others we are passing through an identity crisis.

A recent writer gives a number of reasons for ministry burn out. Two of them are of particular interest when considering ministerial identity. First of all, the pastor is constantly trying to relate to people's expectations of him. He is well aware of what they expect him to be and to do, and of his own failure to achieve. Secondly, the pastor must function a great deal of his time on his persona. Persona has been defined as 'an assumed identity or character.' In psychological terms it is the mechanism that conceals a person's true thoughts or feelings. It means that the pastor is operating behind a mask all the time and seldom, if ever, is able to be his true self.

Both these situations raise the question of identity. On the one hand people know what sort of minister they want or expect and, on the other, the minister is trying to be, very often, what he is not. Identity is, therefore, closely allied to role. Is it something given to us by others and we attempt to fit in or is it something which we are attempting to fulfil which isn't really ourselves? Is our ministry a game of role-playing?

The real trouble is that many modern pastors, for reasons we shall see later, feel that they are being left without a role and are, accordingly, either busy searching for one or trying to claw one back. There are several obvious paths to disaster. We can be confused as to our role. We can adopt the wrong role. We can assume a role which is false and hide behind our persona, constantly acting a part.

The question many of us have struggled with, then, is the identification of our role as pastors. It is helpful to think, initially, of the factors which have either deprived us of our traditional role or caused us confusion as we have attempted to identify it.

Counsellors or pastors?

It is undoubtedly true that the replacement of pastoral care by clinical models has done a great deal to cause bewilderment in pastoral ranks. Particularly in the USA, the pastor has been replaced by the counsellor and his or her 'ministry' has been given priority over pastoral oversight and care, over pastoral praying and preaching and over what used to be called 'the cure of souls.'

Effectiveness in counselling has demanded expertise and techniques, some of them foreign to the pastor. The main problem is, however, that counselling has tended to focus on problems, often identifying them where they have never been recognised.

Several years ago we entertained an American naval chaplain in our home for a few days. He served on a nuclear submarine. He told us that the authorities did not believe that a large number of men could remain happy and contented while they were submerged in a submarine for several months' tour of duty. On his last trip they had been required to ship a psychiatrist and he had concluded that the whole crew were a bunch of neurotic freaks! Years later we fostered a young boy and hence had to cope with frequent visits from a social worker. Soon after David became part of our family, the social worker asked, 'What does he call you?' We had to admit that he had not called us anything so far. Family life, we claimed, could continue on a reasonably satisfactory level without names being used. The next day, however, she telephoned to ask how we were getting on with 'the problem.' We were not aware that it had assumed the proportions of a problem but we were increasingly convinced that the social worker was problem-obsessed.

Problem orientated

Because people are either referred to, or seek out, a counsellor, it is not surprising that counsellors relate to people in terms of their problems. Those who come are either depressed, suffering from bereavement, facing marital breakdown or can't cope. Seeing people in this way stresses the need for expertise and, as pastors, we are made aware of our grave limitations and our lack of suitable training. We know the difference between Calvinism and Arminianism but we have only a hazy knowledge of the different types of depressive illness.

On a deeper level we find that we are relating to people, not in terms of their 'problems' as such, but in terms of their efforts simply to live life. This was brought very strongly home to me when I took a student placement round some church homes one afternoon. At the end he said 'My, you don't half have to cope with some pastoral problems!' I was lost for words until I realised that he was looking for problems whereas I was simply relating to my people and their situations as I found them. Like our foster son's use or otherwise of our names, these people were coping with situations, which they shared with me, which they considered commonplace.

Increasingly the attitude of my placement student and social worker is winning. We look for problems and we refer them to a counsellor or we attempt to be counsellors ourselves rather than pastors.

Derek Tidball puts it perfectly in *Skilful Shepherds*:

...the task of caring has been given into the hands of other professionals. The advent of the secular therapist and the explosion of the social services have been a profound threat to the minister who so often has been made to feel an amateur among other professionals, with little to contribute to the problems of the real world. [1]

The pastor was struggling with a difficult situation in the life of a middle aged man in his congregation. He was party to confidential information that the man was facing the onset of mental illness. Not surprisingly, the man's marriage and family life were being affected. Somehow or other the situation came up in a deacons' meeting. Quick as a flash one deacon, who had done a short counselling course, declared, 'There is nothing in this situation that a good marriage guidance counsellor couldn't solve in five minutes!' By implication the pastor's approach was dismissed and replaced by the 'expert's' advice even though the pastor knew it was wrong. Such remarks imply that the pastor's role is confined to a small religious area in people's lives and that, when he ventures outside that area, he is nothing but a blundering amateur.

The pastor has thus come to be regarded as redundant in areas where he was once useful. As Derek Tidball says: 'It is a long time since he has acted as an officer of the law, or of health, a teacher or a local government administrator.' [2] If a pastor doubts this then he has only to compare his Vestry Hour and its countless requests to sign passport forms and provide references with the needs which get poured out in the average GP's surgery.

Pastor or preacher?

Another factor which has led to an identity crisis is the false separation many have made between pastoral work and preaching. It is not uncommon to hear the assessment, 'He's no preacher but he's an excellent pastor!' Among those ordained to ministerial office there are always those who consider that they are pastors rather than preachers and those who feel that they are more preachers than pastors. The division is often a problem to them and, all too frequently, they don't really know who or what they are. Some, quite wrongly, insist on the division in their ministry. A well known minister, years ago in Edinburgh, was reputed to have said to his congregation, 'You can have my head or my feet!'

Can we, in fact, tolerate that division without running into an identity crisis of the first order? Preaching and pastoral work belong together and are practically synonymous. William Temple wrote, 'The best preaching is a fruit of constant pastoral visiting; it springs out of the relationship between pastor and people.' [3] Years ago the speaker at a ministers' meeting failed to turn up and one present, almost on the spur of the moment, produced a tape of a talk given by a psychiatrist. Many of us present were grateful for that 'substitute' speaker! He spoke of the pastoral impact of systematic Biblical preaching. He stressed that, in the Psalms for example, every human condition and problem could be found. Faithful preaching, he claimed, was essentially pastoral and called on us not to make the division which was so common. 'You are pastors,' he insisted, 'when you are preaching.'

Objections to preaching

Even that assertion raises another problem, that of the contemporary objections to preaching as a means of communication in a television age. In 1857 Anthony Trollope wrote *Barchester Towers*. One of the novel's main characters is the Rev. Obadiah Slope, the chaplain to Bishop Proudie. Slope preaches in the Cathedral and that gives Trollope the opportunity to say:

There is, perhaps, no greater hardship at present inflicted on mankind in civilized and free countries, than the necessity of listening to sermons. No-one but a preaching-clergyman has, in these realms, the power of compelling an audience to sit silent, and be tormented...He is the bore of the age...the nightmare that disturbs our Sunday's rest, the incubus that overloads our religion and makes God's service distasteful. [4]

The modern reaction to preaching is not so much that sermons are boring but that they represent a method of communication which has been superseded by television, the electronic media and the visual image. When I gave notice of a series of sermons on Romans a number of years ago the hope was expressed by one, who claimed to be well educated, that, if I insisted on going ahead, I should use 'lots of illustrations and visual aids.' Sermons also assume an authority of utterance which is at odds with an age of tolerance and pluralism. The pulpit can no longer assume that it is six feet above contradiction. All this has been well worked over by various writers but the pastor, who is, after all, at the sharp edge of things, is acutely aware of the problem. It is brought home to him in ways subtle and, sometimes, not so subtle. In many churches, too, the increasing emphasis on, and interest in, worship has tended to downgrade the place of the sermon despite the insistence of pastors, backed by scholars, that preaching is an essential component of true worship. My wife and I attended a very large renewal conference a number of years ago where the worship was hailed as 'vibrant'. When speakers rose to preach it was impossible to miss the shuffling and general restlessness of large sections of those present.

It is not surprising that the pastor, believing that he possesses a preaching gift, begins to wonder about things and asks some very real questions about his identity as a 'preacher of the Word.'

Team leadership

The problem is compounded when the church in which he serves talks of there being a 'team ministry.' In my denomination there are several churches where there is a preaching rota and the pastoral care is in the hands of a specialised group. All that has much to commend it but where does that leave the ordained minister? Despite his polite silence on the matter he, inwardly, is often in turmoil over the answer. In truth he occasionally feels that the church could function effectively without him.

So, in the midst of this all too common confusion, what are we?

It helps to realise, to begin with, that though the majority of the early Christians were Jews, they totally neglected the idea of a separate group within their ranks, akin to the priesthood among the ancient Jewish people of God. It is no exaggeration to say that all the early Christians were lay people. It would be more accurate, however, to say that they were all ministers. As the people of God they all had a ministry, a function within the body of Christ. They were a society of ministers, serving their Lord, ministering to the world and one another.

If all were ministers not all, however, had the same type of ministry. There were different types or functions as Paul teaches quite clearly in Romans 12, 1 Corinthians 12 and Ephesians 4. What these passages teach is that every Christian has a gift, a 'ministry', but no one Christian is expected to possess and practise all the gifts. Far from accelerating the redundancy of the ordained minister, or catapulting him into a debilitating identity crisis, these truths point the way to his principal function. It is by preaching, encouragement, and whatever other means at his disposal, that he trains and facilitates the other 'ministers' in the exercise of their gifts in the church and in society. He is a resource person carrying out an equipping ministry. Instead of calling him the 'minister' or 'pastor' he could properly be called the coach. 'The glory of the coach' writes Elton Trueblood, 'is that of being the discoverer, the developer, the trainer of the powers of other men.' [5] His responsibility, as coach in the local church, is not to hog the limelight and stand on a lonely and superior pedestal, but to do, with every member, what his Master did with a little group of ordinary men who eventually were charged with turning the world upside down.

When these truths are recognised, and accepted, the pastor will no longer feel threatened by the existence of a team or preaching rota. No longer will he go quickly on the defensive to guard his own little corner and dampen down the gifts of others. He will glory in the gifts he recognises in the lives of others and will see his calling in life to be the development and encouragement of ministries which function differently from his own. A coach who coaches seldom has an identity crisis! A pastor who denies the existence of the ministry of others usually has a whopping one! [6]

So we are 'coaches' or 'facilitators.'

Men of God

In a unique way we are also to be men of God.

Frederic Greeves in his *Theology and the Cure of Souls*, writing of the doctor who calls in the pastor, says, 'Doctors want the minister's help precisely because he is not a psychiatrist, but a minister...unfortunately it is probably true that the vast majority of the medical profession does not know what it is really that ministers can do.' [7] That contention was borne out several years ago when I was attending a conference, convened by a hospice, on co-operation between doctors and clergy. At one point one of the GPs present challenged one of the clergy: 'I would refer patients to you if I knew what you were expert in!'

Frank Wright claims that the pastor must have 'not so much a claim to uniqueness or distinctiveness, as the challenge to a task.' Quoting an eminent church leader he goes on to define that task as seeking 'to keep the mystery of God present to man.' [8]

How would that GP have reacted to the reply 'We are experts in God!'? Frederic Greeves would have replied in that way. 'There are very many people trying to help those with troubled minds; but how few there are who have time to talk to them about God.' [9] When he was Archbishop of Canterbury, Donald Coggan addressed Wesley College, Leeds, at its Inaugural Service in 1966 with these words:

How can a man be an evangelist, a counsellor, a visitor, a preacher, unless he be essentially a "man of God"? His evangelism will strike a hollow note; his counselling will be merely good advice (although perhaps flavoured with psychiatric phraseology or even the odd text of Scripture); his visiting will tend to deal only with the weather or the cricket score; his preaching will be mere talk, though maybe talk with expert techniques; unless the man himself be, in very fact, a man of God.[10]

In a recent public discussion a prominent Christian academic expressed his distaste of people who, because they were 'ordained', claimed to have a hot line to God. If such people claimed to have, precisely because of some ceremony, a unique relationship to God then the stricture was legitimate. What, hopefully, he was not objecting to was the fact that the pastor's unique responsibility is to make sure that God is introduced to every sphere of human life and every dimension of human experience whether good or bad. When he relates to people, his primary task is to enable them to turn away from themselves, and especially from what threatens, to the God who loves and saves.

Narcissism

Such a priority is at odds with the current secular emphasis. People have almost been completely deceived into being preoccupied with themselves. It is even the thrust of many Christian 'how-to' books. They place the emphasis on the human initiative, the human method, the human answer and season it all with a sprinkling of spirituality. The pastor, as a man of God, has another emphasis, that of directing folk in trouble to the God who cares and heals. Someone has said, 'The curse of the contemporary emphasis on personal growth is its narcissism: the secret of sanctification is the abandonment of every attempt to cultivate the self, or in a still simpler formula, coming from the heart of the gospel, it is losing ourselves to find ourselves.'

As pastors, we are never more completely ourselves, or what we should be, than when we are signposts to the God we serve.

If as men of God we find our true identity in pointing our people to God then we also find ourselves when we are seen to be men of God, or Godly, in life and character. Paul addressed young Timothy as 'But you, man of God...' (1 Timothy 6:11). It will come over, as Paul suggests in that context, in what we 'flee' and in our obedience 'without spot or blame' (6:14). Perhaps Robert Murray McCheyne had that passage in mind when he wrote: 'My people's greatest need is my personal holiness.'[11]

Sadly, here again such an emphasis is strangely at odds with modern demands of the minister. Many a vacancy committee will look for skills and abilities before they look for sanctity. They deserve, all too often, the rebuke of one college principal to a vacancy committee after they had outlined what they perceived to be the principal needs of the area. 'You are looking for a social worker. I can only offer you a man of God.' Listen to Frederic Greeves again:

When men and women discover that a minister lives in close touch with God, is able to help them love God, cares for them with something of the care of Jesus, and ministers to them in holy things, they do not find it very difficult to think of him as "*the* minister".[12]

Shepherds
If we are men of God then we are also shepherds.

Here we must be careful. To describe the pastor as a shepherd clearly rings bells in a farming community but means little to those who live in one of today's concrete jungles. When we talk of the pastor's role in terms of care and that, to many, is what a shepherd does, then we have to accept that many a doctor, social or community worker and nurse fulfils the same function in a needy society. Yet the figure is biblical and can properly be used to clarify a minister's identity. The passages in the Gospels where Jesus sees himself as a shepherd are well known and equally well understood. The metaphor which is used of our Lord is applied to one form of Christian ministry in Ephesians 4:11 where the same Greek word is translated 'pastor'. The noun is not used of ministers elsewhere in the New Testament but the cognate verb is used twice. Paul, in his farewell address to the elders of the church in Ephesus, encourages them to act as shepherds to the church. Peter instructs another group of elders to tend the flock of God which is in their charge (Acts 20:28; 1 Peter 5:2).

If we are hesitant about the term then we can certainly identify the responsibility of the person who is called a shepherd and examine the function.

Augustine describes his function as follows:

Disturbers are to be rebuked, the low-spirited are to be encouraged, the infirm to be supported, objectors confuted, the treacherous guarded against, the unskilled taught, the lazy roused, the contentious restrained, the haughty repressed, litigants pacified, the poor relieved, the oppressed liberated, the good approved, the evil borne with and all are to be loved. [13]

Richard Baxter identifies a number of people to whom the minister will relate in his pastoral role.

'The first part of our ministerial work lieth in bringing unsound professors of the faith to sincerity, that they who before were Christians in name and show, may be so indeed...IT belong to us, as their pastors, to convert these seeming Christians to sincerity, because such seeming Christians may be visible members of our churches.' So we have a role in relation to nominal Christians within our churches and that, sadly, means that we are not short of a job!

Secondly, Baxter identifies the building up of those already converted as part of our pastoral role. We have to concentrate on the weak and the immature.

Baxter identifies the third group as 'those that labour under some particular distemper, which keeps under their graces and makes them temptations and troubles to others and a burden to themselves...' These 'tempers' he identifies as pride, worldliness, sensual desire and disturbing passions. They sound old-fashioned terms but most modern pastors will be able to identify them in contemporary flocks of Christian sheep!

The fourth group are the backsliders '...that are either fallen into some scandalous sin, or else abate their zeal and diligence, and shew us that they have lost their former love.' Sadly such folk are far from rare in our modern church rolls.

Baxter then deals with the pastor's relation to 'those who have fallen under some great temptation' and insists that 'every minister should be a man that hath much insight into the tempter's wiles.' [14]

If we accept what Baxter says about the work of the shepherd then the average faithful minister will find little difficulty in discovering his role and, with it, his identity. The only caveat which I must add is to insist that he works alongside other 'shepherds' in the church. Here, again, his responsibility will be that of a facilitator enabling the members of the church to be caring and supportive in their relationships. If the pastor begins to see networks of care in the church and gives them his support then he will be a true shepherd of the flock. If, on the other hand, he insists that he must be the only source of pastoral care, and seeks to exercise it totally by himself, he will not only exhaust himself but he will also encounter acute frustration. One man bands attract spectators—and who wants a church of spectators?

The minister's role and sense of identity are certainly under attack. The source of the attack lies deep in the culture in which we have to exercise our ministry. It doesn't help either that, all too often, he is the butt of humour. In Scotland the influence of the television figure of the Rev. IM Jolly has been erosive. Yet, once we begin to think of what God calls us to we begin to realise that we have a unique role to play in Christ's Body.

Discouragement

One of the most crucial battles of the Second World War was about to be fought in the North African desert. The British Eighth Army had gone forward before, many times, but had always been pushed back. They had really got nowhere. They were hopelessly discouraged, that is, until General Bernard Montgomery took over their command.

On the eve of the Battle of El Alamein in October 1942, General Montgomery pinned on the door of his headquarters the words prayed by Sir Frances Drake many years previously, before he too joined battle with the enemy.

O Lord God, when Thou givest to Thy servants to endeavour any great matter, grant us to know that it is not the beginning but the continuing of the same, until it is thoroughly finished which yieldeth the true glory.

The Eighth Army and their friends went on to finish the job and enjoy the glory. Most of us, however, have been tempted to give up the job in hand, to relinquish some daunting challenge or to surrender some heavy responsibility. We have quite simply become discouraged.

Few in Christian ministry or leadership have escaped. Gripped by discouragement there have been many, sadly, over the years who have given up altogether and resigned. Gifted and able preachers have vacated their pulpits and gone silent. Missionaries, burdened, initially, by concern for some country and its people have come home and settled for a quiet life.

Others have continued to go through the motions of Christian ministry but the effects of discouragement have been no less obvious. There is a conscious lowering of standards in sermon preparation, a less rigorous life of personal devotion, a strange indifference to the need to give biblical and visionary leadership to a church and a general lowering of expectations and hopes. When a stand is called for against some wrong there is either a token objection or a sinful silence. Vigour of commitment and action are replaced by a willingness to let things slide or drift and instead of striding forward, the pastor finds every excuse for the easy chair of inactivity if not indolence. Surrender to discouragement is not easily hidden.

The sources of discouragement

The causes, or sources, of discouragement are almost too numerous to mention and are often personal to the individual concerned. What discourages one servant of God can be seen by another as a challenge to be faced and overcome. It is important, therefore, to realise that psychological or personality factors may well be involved. Having said that, several well established sources of discouragement have been identified over the years.

We can think, first of all, of the constant obstacles and problems which seem to afflict all who would serve Christ's Kingdom.

Paul, for example, was no stranger to opposition and rejection. At Iconium 'There was a plot afoot among the Gentiles and Jews, together with their leaders, to ill-treat (Paul and Barnabas) and stone them. But they found out about it and fled to the Lycaonian cities of Lystra and Derbe and to the surrounding country, where they continued to preach the good news' (Acts 14:5,6). That was no isolated, one-off incident but the pattern of Paul's evangelism. The cause for thanksgiving is that, instead of giving up, discouraged by the unremitting opposition, he moved on and kept on preaching the Word.

The reaction of Paul and his companion stands in striking contrast to that of many another servant of God. Opposition is unrelenting. Criticism is a steady, chilling drip. Obstruction is the order of the day. Every suggestion or idea is vetoed often without rational explanation. A member of a committee can be consistently negative. Not surprisingly, profound discouragement sets in. It becomes debilitating. A once-effective ministry comes slowly to an end. It is true that the opposition can come from a group, often with vested interests. Friends in Christian ministry, sharing their problems, have identified the source as a group of Masons within the leadership or those, long established within a fellowship, who are firmly opposed to change. A few, frequently linked by marriage, can form an effective and resolute blocking group.

Again, it can be just one individual. Paul tells Timothy that 'Alexander the metalworker did me a great deal of harm'. He goes on to warn his young friend 'You too should be on your guard against him, because he strongly opposed our message' (2 Timothy 4:15). The presence of a similar Alexander, much given to throwing buckets of cold, discouraging water over the pastor, can be an all too familiar experience.

William Carey, the father of the modern missionary movement, was no stranger to obstacles and problems. 'When I first left England' he wrote, 'my hope of the conversion of the heathen was very strong, but among so many obstacles it would utterly die away, having nothing to cherish it but many things to obstruct it, unless upheld by God'. [1] Most pastors could have written these words.

The idol of success

Success is the great idol of today. Even in Christian circles it is admired and used as the evidence of true effectiveness. 'Since the Rev Joe Bloggs became the pastor of X its membership has trebled.' What are we to make of that? When the pastor of some struggling fellowship hears it he knows pangs of acute discouragement. He, too, has been hard working, diligent in prayer, faithful in his ministry but, if numbers are the touchstone of success, he has missed out. He is left discouraged and questioning. The modern penchant for success stories, often appearing in print and becoming best sellers, and sometime narrated in great rallies to appreciative listeners, contributes to the sum total of discouragement. The Church Growth movement, in its less than sophisticated forms, must bear some of the responsibility here. We are far, hopefully, from published league tables of growing churches but numbers have become important.

Not far removed from the discouragement associated with an emphasis on success is the discouragement associated with the failure to produce instant results and solutions. Eugene Peterson, in *A Long Obedience In The Same Direction* expresses the problem perfectly:

I don't know what it has been like for pastors in other cultures and previous centuries, but I am quite sure that for a pastor in Western culture in the latter part of the twentieth century the aspect of *world* that makes the work of leading Christians in the way of faith most difficult is what Gore Vidal has analysed as "today's passion for the immediate and the casual". Everyone is in a hurry. The persons, whom I lead in worship, among whom I counsel, visit, pray, preach, and teach, want short cuts. They want me to help them fill out the form that will get them instant credit (in eternity). They are impatient for results. They have adopted the lifestyle of a tourist and only want the high spots. [2]

Many a pastor will bluntly admit that sheer lack of support is the source of his growing discouragement. He stresses the priority of prayer and attendance at prayer meetings. The majority of the leadership are conspicuous by their absence. He encourages evangelism both by his teaching and example. His people seem indifferent. He spells out the spiritual enrichment likely to be received at some convention. His folk stay away in droves. He preaches his heart out and the result is stony silence. 'Why do I bother?' expresses the exasperation of discouragement.

So we could go on and, the more we do so, the more we run the danger of talking ourselves into a dark discouragement. Not before time we now have to ask, 'How do we deal with discouragement from whatever source?' On a Monday morning, with a profitless Sunday's preaching behind us, or tossing in bed after a negative and far from constructive committee, what direction ought our minds to take?

God's call and commission

Before discouragement gets the upper hand there must be a reaffirmation within us of God's call and commission. We are where we are, with all that may involve, because God called us and put us there. That truth is not just the bottom line; it is the top line too.

Leighton Ford, Billy Graham's brother-in-law, is fond of telling how, in 1960, his plane touched down briefly in Dakar, West Africa. A French missionary, who had laboured in that Muslim area for ten years, had coffee with him during the brief stop over. To the question 'How many converts have you had?' he replied 'One, two—perhaps three'. 'Why do you stay?' was the further question. 'I stay because Jesus Christ put me here'. [3] It is all too easy to forget that truth. We start our ministry among our people with all the right ideas. Discouragements begin to appear. We all too quickly begin to think of moving on. Eugene Peterson in *Under the Unpredictable Plant* insists, rightly, that 'a congregation is not a job site to be abandoned when a better offer comes along'. [4] Yet, is the fact of God's call to work in a certain area and among a particular group of people something to be discarded lightly when things get troublesome? Far from it. We are there, among those who are negative and obstructive, daily faced with indifference and lack of response, ministering, not to growing crowds, but to a handful of ordinary folk, because God's will is that we should be there and we obeyed. In that call we were not promised an easy ride. Even if we didn't realise to the full the implications of his call, God did and he still chose and appointed us. We are his obedient servants, not spiritual fly-by-nights.

God's call provided the steel and resolution in Paul's ministry. Writing to the Corinthians, he is about to describe the hardships and suffering involved in Christian service. He will freely admit that he is a 'jar of clay' and, therefore, prone to all the feelings, including discouragement, which can come to a mere human being under pressure. Yet he begins the chapter (2 Corinthians 4) with the ringing affirmation 'Therefore, since through God's mercy we have this ministry, we do not lose heart'.

Sometimes we shall have to say that strongly and forcibly to ourselves. On other occasions a faithful spouse or a faithful friend will say it to us. The rebuke will be sharp but it will be our salvation. Discouragement is choked by the reaffirmation of the fact that we are where we are because God called and commissioned us.

Proper sowing

The onset of feelings of discouragement may need, from time to time, the rediscovery of faithfulness. So much in Scripture points to this. Of course the farmer hopes for a good harvest, in the same way as the pastor hopes and prays for numbers responding, but his first responsibility is to sow the seed. 'God makes it grow' (1 Corinthians 3:7). It was TS Eliot who said 'Take no thought of harvest but only of proper sowing'. So, when we are tempted to be distracted into the dark valley of discouragement by so much that we experience and by so many whom we encounter, we have to rediscover our priority. It is to sow—and that requires perseverance despite stony unresponsive ground, choking weeds and the rest. The trouble is that we have a very human, and understandable, desire to see change resulting from our work but, as someone once said, 'if our gratification has to come from visible change, we have made God into a businessman and ourselves into sales managers'. We are humble sowers of seed. It is Almighty God who gives the growth. The growth will certainly come, perhaps not in our time, perhaps not in the way we envisage, but it will come by God's grace, in his time and to his glory. Our faith gives us that assurance. The seed of the Word of God is not sterile.

An illustration of this truth is instructive. Henry Martyn lived a short life (from 1781 till 1812) but a quite remarkable one. In 1805 he went to India as a chaplain to the East India Company and gave himself to the laborious task of translating the New Testament and Book of Common Prayer into Hindustani. Later, shortly before his death, he completed the Arabic and Persian translation of the New Testament. Suffering as he did from tuberculosis, he could easily have been discouraged by the nature of the work. Yet faithfulness refused to allow discouragement a foothold. In a letter he wrote, 'I think I am willing to continue throwing the net at the Lord's command all the long night of life, though the end may be that I shall have caught nothing'.[5] What God required of, and received from, Henry Martyn was faithfulness. He was prepared to accept a situation which would have discouraged many another person. Yet, from the vantage point of history, we can see the results and the way God used that man to his glory.

Billy Graham has often made the same point of his own ministry. God has granted him the privilege of seeing people responding when he has preached but he has insisted that he has simply been reaping where others, tempted to be discouraged at times, have done the faithful, and often backbreaking, sowing.

God's call and our faithfulness go together. God has put us where we are and our response is to be faithful in the execution of that call. If we are blessed by numbers and a bountiful harvest, then we shall give God the glory. If we are not, then we just keep doing what God requires of us—sowing, knowing that the harvest will come in God's time and way.

Rededication to the humdrum

Discouragement will also find it difficult to grow if there is in us a constant rededication to the humdrum. That isn't easy in a society which is easily bored, likes the dramatic and feeds on the sensational. Even in

Christian circles there is a suspicion that Christians need the exciting, the novel and the different. The ordinary is lightly esteemed and even dismissed. The young people of a friend's church attended a youth rally a number of years ago on a Saturday night in a city some distance away. It was exciting, drawing on all the resources of a multi-media presentation. There was a modern music group and the speaking was dramatic with powerful illustrations. 'You've met real Christianity here tonight', the speaker claimed. 'Compare it with the dull services in your local church tomorrow!'

You cannot help wondering if the speaker that night could have coped with the week in, week out, committed and loving slog required of my ministerial friend. He had refused to be discouraged by the problems and difficulties involved in working in a council estate with few committed resources. He was prepared to do his work faithfully, pray diligently and wait patiently for God to move. He was annoyed, but not put off, by the arrogance of the speaker in Edinburgh. He saw the routine, almost humdrum, work of preaching Sunday by Sunday and the steady visitation of the homes in the estate as what God had called him to do and he did it faithfully.

A vicar in Aston, Birmingham ended a letter to John Robinson, then Bishop of Woolwich, with these words: 'I am not reaping a harvest; I scarcely claim to be sowing the seed; I am hardly ploughing the soil; but I am gathering out the stones'.[6] That is the attitude which banishes discouragement. It turns its back on the demand for the extraordinary, the dramatic or even the sensational and is prepared to do what has to be done at that time, leaving the future to God. William Temple somewhere wrote 'Of all the work that produces results nine-tenths must be drudgery. There is no work from the lowest to the highest which can be done well by the man who is unwilling to make that sacrifice'.

Faithful perseverance

A longing for the Christian equivalent of the bright lights and the dramatic will inevitably breed in any pastor restlessness, discontent and profound discouragement. It is the man who is prepared to keep at it, to slog away, to cope with the routine and apparently humdrum and to be faithful in the everyday responsibilities of ministry who will be a stranger to discouragement. Not that he will be a lover and promoter of boredom. He will attempt to make his presentation attractive and use whatever modern resources are available to him but his emphasis will be on faithful perseverance. He will sympathise with what Christopher Columbus felt like on his epic voyage. His crew wanted to turn back. Every day seemed the same. Yet Columbus wrote in his log 'Sailed on!' He reached the New World. Discouragement gets us nowhere.

On one occasion Martin Luther's wife came to him and, obviously dejected, said to him, 'Have you heard the terrible news? God is dead!' Deeply shocked, he rebuked her blasphemous words. 'And if God is not dead', she retorted, 'what right have you, his servant, you a Christian man, to be so downcast and depressed?' A great Christian echoed the same truth when he said 'A Christian man has no right to be discouraged in the same world as God'.

We thus can identify surely the greatest antidote to discouragement. It is the belief that God is alive, active and working out his sovereign and loving purposes. It is the belief that in this broken and rebellious world God is working out his saving will through a sufficient Saviour. It is the belief that, in this community where so many seem to reject him, he will still glorify his name. It is the belief that, in this difficult spot where God has placed me, he is active and powerful, he is sitting on a throne. He is neither wringing his hands in helplessness nor is he withdrawn in indifference.

It could be claimed that we are the victims, all too often, of a devil inspired deception. So much in society pressurises us, even as Christians and even as Christian leaders, to think of ourselves. We become obsessed with our feelings and reactions, our moods and our attitudes. We think of our aspirations and hopes and what we are doing and what we hope to achieve. We are then puzzled and disturbed when we become discouraged or experience some other debilitating emotion. Is it any wonder when our starting point is self? As we have ended by thinking of God, his sovereignty and his purposes; it could well be that we should have started there. For, when our minds start with thinking deeply of God, when we work simply to do his will and when we are captivated by his greatness and saving power we shall wonder, if we ever think about it at all, what discouragement is all about. 'For from him and through him and to him are all things. To him be the glory for ever!' (Romans 11:36).

Criticism

A n infection which developed during a period in hospital proved devastating. Of little comfort was the observation of a doctor friend: 'What did you expect? Hospitals are alive with bugs!'

It would be easy to come to the same conclusion about some churches. The most common of the bugs, and by far the most unpleasant, is the spirit of criticism. Whether it is of the choice of Sunday's hymns, the quality of the musicians, the efficiency of those responsible for the amplification, the decisions of the elders or deacons, or the preacher or the preaching—so it goes on and on and is as debilitating as any hospital bug. Many a pastor feels helpless, and even angry, when he realises how firm a grip this particular germ has on his people. No one seems exempt. Certainly those, including himself, who are committed, who accept responsibility and who give of themselves wholeheartedly, appear to be the principal targets. 'Censure', said Jonathan Swift, 'is the tax a man pays to the public for being eminent'. An older pastor used to claim that the three pre-requisites of a pastor were a large waste paper basket, a sense of humour and a hide like a rhinoceros. Unfortunately the critical wounding letters cannot always be consigned to the bin or the shredder, the sense of humour becomes exhausted and the skin is often thinner than we would like. The unfairness of it all lies partly in the fact that those who criticise are usually those on the fringe, who stand back and are deaf to every appeal for service.

Nor does lack of knowledge inhibit the critic. Harold Macmillan, a former Prime Minister of the United Kingdom, once said, 'I have never found in a long experience of politics that criticism is ever inhibited by ignorance'. You do not need to pastor a Christian fellowship, sadly, to come to the same conclusion.

Cheap superiority

The criticism bug is a master of disguise. Though it may be a lie it often strikes camouflaged with outraged piety. The critic often adopts a lofty pose. It was James Denney, the Scottish theologian, who wrote in one of his commentaries, 'The natural man loves to find fault; it gives him at the cheapest rate the comfortable feeling of superiority'. Criticism, all too often, can be cut-price superiority coming, not from a natural man, but from a professing believer.

Valued criticism

It must be said that not all criticism is bad and not all critics are to be resented. When criticism comes as a bug it has to be dealt with firmly. When it comes as informed assessment, with the aim of correction, then it deserves to be taken seriously and acted upon. That pastor would be a fool who rejected every word which assessed his work negatively. It is said that when Dawson Trotman, founder of the Navigators, was criticised, he prayed: 'Lord, please show me the kernel of truth hidden in this criticism'. Paul's advice to the Galatians is wise: 'Brothers, if someone is caught in a sin, you who are spiritual should restore him gently'. Paul, interestingly, is aware of the danger in being a 'restoring' critic so he goes on: 'But watch yourself, or you also may be tempted' (Galatians 6:1).

This writer, at one point in his early ministry, became more and more involved in a church building project. He will always be grateful to the elder brother who drew him to one side and gently suggested that the lay members of the church could choose the fittings and the furniture: 'We're happy to do that but we have set you apart during the week to concentrate on your pastoral work and pulpit preparation'. It was a wise and necessary word of restoration to the pastor's unique calling. To reject or resent it would have been insensitive and disastrous.

It still has to be faced that, in general, the spirit of criticism in a Christian fellowship is destructive rather than restorative. Ill-informed criticism can do immense damage. It can ruin confidence, stimulate cynicism, provoke exasperation and produce resignations. Sleepless nights can be due, not to over-active minds, but to spirits wounded by carefully directed barbs and cruel and thoughtless criticisms. A member of the congregation almost caused withdrawal from the Christian ministry by the bold statement to her pastor: 'You lack integrity!' No criticism could be more fundamental. When later challenged she claimed that she had no ground for the charge but she had made it in order to test his reaction. Little did she know the heart searching and sleepless agony her pastor, and his wife, had endured.

Again, it has to be noted that, in church families where the adults have a reputation for criticism, the children have a tendency to lapse from attendance and commitment. It is not difficult to understand the reason. Why attend something which is so poor in their parents' eyes? Why accept the truth when the messenger is fit only to be carved to bits? Scripture has severe warnings for those who cause 'these little ones to stumble'. Negative and critical parents have a lot to answer for.

Why so common?

Why is it that this bug has such a hold on professing Christians? Why is it that so many within our churches are so ready to wound and hurt with their criticisms? The usual answer is that Christians are still human, the fallen sons and daughters of Adam. Those who criticise will not be perfect until they reach heaven and so we can expect to encounter barbs and hurtful comments, unfounded and unfair criticism. If this is true, and it is, what then do we make of the assertion by Paul that the love of God is shed abroad in our hearts by the Holy Spirit? Has that glorious truth no effect on our attitude and relationship to other Christians, what we are to believe about them and how we talk about them? 'Love one another' seems a straight-forward enough command but does cruel, unremitting criticism sit well with it? If the local fellowship is part of the Body of Christ, indwelt by his Spirit and purchased with his blood, should its members not be slow to carve it to pieces?

There seems a remarkable inconsistency between the prevalence of criticism within the church and the teaching of Scripture on the nature of the church and how its members ought to relate.

When a young believer says of a prominent family within the church: 'The criticism of the church starts before I am properly across their doorstep,' is that family not sinning against the nature of Christ's Body? We have every right to expect that love should inhibit thoughtless, ill-informed criticism, hasty judgments and unfeeling barbs. We ought to expect that a weak and struggling fellowship should receive the under-standing and forgiveness due to part of the Body of Christ.

Given, then, that criticism will come, how should we react?

Part of our reaction should be to ask what lies behind it. One preacher friend admitted that often in the margin of his sermon manuscript he would mark in red ink 'Shout here—argument weak!' Is the dedicated critic shouting because he knows there is something wrong in his own life? Is his commitment to criticism a defence mechanism or a confession that he has found that attack is the best method of defence?

When, for some, the preached truth hurts then their learned response is to criticise the hymns or the musicians or the preacher's style or their fellow Christians. The pastor's task will be to probe, gently, but firmly to find the area of sensitivity. That will not be easy. It may well be that, in the past, there has been some unfortunate incident, some breakdown of relationships, some unwise decision which warps and distorts attitudes in the present. To deal with it, years later, can be difficult and require great sensitivity but that is the pastor's calling. He may well have to challenge the perpetual critic with his or her habit. That could be bruising and is best done in the company of another mature Christian.

A reason uncovered

Sometimes the cause is not spiritual but physical or emotional. One leader had a well developed reputation for always being 'against the pastor'. Nothing the pastor could do was right. Finding it both trying and dispiriting, the pastor eventually found out from the man's wife that they were no longer having a sexual relationship due to the difficult birth of their only child. The frustration of that rejection, and the lack of fulfilment which sprang from it, had gradually produced a soured and twisted personality who made others, particularly those who seemed happy, suffer. Perhaps the pastor should have faced the man with his problem. He didn't, and in that he presumably failed, but understanding the situation led to allowances being made and lessened the hurt at some of the more unreasonable criticisms.

Another response to constant criticism is to welcome it! Whenever we are seen to react indignantly to the barbs, we are telling the critic that he has identified a sensitive area in our lives. He knows where to target in the future and does so with deadly accuracy. Much better that we react by assuring the critic that we appreciate his concern for an area which the church leaders have been examining for some time. 'I understand that you have expressed criticisms of what has been happening in the church. We are always concerned to do what is right before God. Will you share with me what you feel has gone wrong? I want to listen to you so that we can learn together to do things properly'. Immediately the critic is made to feel the unity of Christ's Body. Confrontation and division have given way to unity and togetherness.

Confess your faults

A counter-measure against the critic is for the church leader to take the lead in self-criticism. 'Confess your faults to one another' says Scripture and the wise leader does just that. He is quick to climb down from his pedestal and admit that he has made a mistake. He refuses to stand on his dignity and is not slow to admit his own inadequacy. The leadership group refuses to adopt an infallible posture and readily appeals for wisdom and guidance from the other members of the church. One of the greatest dangers facing a leadership group within a Christian fellowship is to believe that they are always right. That attitude will invite growing, and justifiable, criticism. A little biblical humility will help the situation considerably! One writer has said, 'If we examine our own eyes for beams and ruthlessly cast them out, we can spare ourselves some criticism and others the unwelcome task of offering it'.

Silence is a formidable weapon against sharp and unloving criticism. The reaction of silence is wrong when the criticism expressed publicly has point and ought to be taken seriously. When, however, the criticism is expressed in obviously unloving terms and is seen by the rest of the company to be abusive and cruel, then silence, or the turning of the other cheek, is both scriptural and effective. Silence becomes the refusal to descend to the level of the critic. If, after we have searched our hearts, we feel that our consciences are clear, it is often best to make no attempt to justify ourselves. Our Lord, unjustly accused, was silent before his accusers (Mark 14:61).

Prayer changes things

A profitable reaction to criticism is to pray for the critic. Sometimes, it must be said, as we pray we begin to realise just how deserved is much of the criticism and our prickly sensitivity gives way to humble confession. It remains true, however, that prayer for the critic will often lead to awareness, on their part, of what they are really doing, to an appreciation of how censorious and judgmental they have been, and to a new openness to Christ's love. If prayer changes things then the critic can be changed.

A woman was an unrelenting and cruel critic of the pastor and the other leaders of the church. Some of it was expressed to other Christians, a great deal, tragically, to unbelievers at her place of work, and some aired at the congregational meetings of her church. Many were undoubtedly turned away from the Kingdom by her strictures and the atmosphere at the Church Meeting was tense and anxious when she appeared. The pastor, with some initial hesitation, began to take seriously the promise in Matthew 16:19 that 'whatever we bind on earth will be bound in heaven'. So he prayed that the Lord would bind her. She never returned to the meeting of church members. She resigned soon afterwards. Was he right? He believed that he had taken God's word seriously as he prayed.

David and Cush

We know next to nothing of Cush the Benjamite but what we suspect is that he had criticised David and made allegations against him. People like this are to be found in every age. David's reaction in Psalm 7 is instructive. He hurries immediately to God whom he sees as his refuge (1-2), his judge (3-9) and his shield (10-17). David then examines his own heart in verses 3 and 4 ('if I have done this and there is guilt on my hands—if I have done evil to him who is at peace with me or without cause have robbed my foe'). David then, having looked closely at himself, puts his trust completely in his God and concludes that evil recoils on those who are responsible for it. 'He who is pregnant with evil and conceives trouble gives birth to disillusionment. He who digs a hole and scoops it out falls into the pit he has made. The trouble he causes recoils on himself; his violence comes down on his own head' (14-16).

Paul's reaction

An illustration of how criticism was dealt with in the New Testament church will be helpful. You cannot read Paul's Corinthian correspondence without realising that the apostle was the target for severe criticism from some of its members. They compared him unfavourably, for example, with those whom he calls 'the super-apostles'. Early in the second letter he faces up to the charge of unreliability. This criticism was based on the fact that he had changed his travel plans and had not come to see them as he had promised. 'He's a right Yes and No man' was the initial charge. 'That apostle Paul! You can't depend on him!' The criticism went even further. The Corinthians were claiming that if you couldn't depend on his word how could you depend on Paul's teaching. Both Paul, as a man, and the gospel he preached could not be trusted.

These were serious criticisms and not to be taken lightly. If you can point the finger, with justification, at a preacher's untrustworthiness and lack of dependability, what reason do you have for believing that what he preaches is worthy of trust?

Paul defended himself and his reply is instructive (2 Corinthians 1:12 - 2: 4). Firstly he insists that he has a clear conscience (1:12). Other people might be driven by 'worldly wisdom' or 'calculating selfishness'. He believed, however, that the motivating or driving force of his actions reflected the outgoing, unselfish grace of God (12b).

Later on he shows exactly what this means in practice. Yes, he had changed his travel plans, not because he felt like it or it suited him, but because he really cared for them (1:23 - 2:4). If he had come, as he had originally promised, he would have done so wielding the heavy rod of rebuke, such was their behaviour (1 Corinthians 4:21). He had delayed coming in order to give them time to put their house in order and so that their eventual meeting would be cordial. His motive, therefore, was utterly sincere. His actions were dictated by unselfish, gracious concern for their spiritual welfare. His only fault was that he cared for them deeply (2 Corinthians 2:4).

Paul then goes on to insist that, just as he is trustworthy, motivated as he is by Godly grace, so his message can be trusted completely. There is nothing vacillating or unreliable about the Christ of the Gospel. 'For the Son of God, Jesus Christ, who was preached among you by me and Silas and Timothy, was not, "Yes" and "No", but in him it has always been "Yes"' (1:19).

What the apostle's experience is saying to us here is that when we conduct ourselves 'in the holiness and sincerity that are from God' (1:12) and when our motives are a reflection of the unselfish grace of God then, no matter how we are criticised, our conscience can be clear and we uphold and confirm the reliability of the Gospel of Christ.

Suffering unjustly

Perhaps the place to find help when we are criticised without cause is before the cross of our Saviour. Let one experience illustrate this truth. During the handling of a difficult and sensitive issue in a church one of those who disagreed with the leaders questioned their motives and implied non-existent malice and enmity. The leaders were surprised and shaken. Shortly afterwards one of them attended a home Bible Study. The passage under discussion was that in Peter's first Epistle dealing with the reactions of slaves when they suffered unjustly (1 Peter 2:18-25). If ever scripture came alive it did that night. 'It is commendable if a man bears up under the pain of unjust suffering because he is conscious of God, but if you suffer for doing good and you endure it, this is commendable before God. To this you were called, because Christ suffered for you, leaving you an example, that you should follow in his steps.....When they hurled their insults at him, he did not retaliate; when he suffered, he made no threats. Instead, he entrusted himself to him who judges justly'.

There is only one refuge when you believe yourself to be criticised unjustly and that is beneath the cross of Christ. The matter can safely be left with him.

Loneliness

There is often a positive dimension to the problems which a pastor encounters. We have already seen this to be true with criticism. It can, and often is, wounding and discouraging; but it can also be constructive and creative. So it is with loneliness. It can be debilitating in the extreme yet who would doubt the benefit of 'being alone with God'? Luke tells us that 'Jesus often withdrew to lonely places and prayed' (Luke 5:16). Christians, of all ages and in all generations, have followed their Master in this and have withdrawn, simply to be alone and to wait upon God.

We find illustrations of the same aloneness long before the model of our Lord's earthly ministry. 'When Moses went up on the mountain, the cloud covered it, and the glory of the Lord settled on Mount Sinai. For six days the cloud covered the mountain, and on the seventh day the Lord called to Moses from within the cloud. To the Israelites the glory of the Lord looked like a consuming fire on top of the mountain. Then Moses entered the cloud as he went on up the mountain. And he stayed on the mountain forty days and forty nights' (Exodus 24:15-18). Moses was alone for over a month, but his face was to shine as a result. It could be that the permanent frown or worried look would disappear from our faces if we spent more time on a mountain alone with God! Jacob was another whose life was to be transformed by an experience with no other human being present. His life-changing experience was to take place when he sent ahead his wives, concubines, children and all others connected with him and was alone, with a stranger, at the Brook Jabbok.

Even pastors can be slow, even wary, of exchanging their frequent loneliness of responsibility and concern for the aloneness of encounter and renewal. There is a strong suspicion that pastors can be woefully negligent in setting apart time to be alone with God, so caught up are they in the fast pace of modern ministerial life. One colleague, doing some research for a project on spirituality, was disturbed to find that only a small proportion of fellow pastors sampled acknowledged that they practised daily Bible reading and prayer. What these suspicions and findings point to is a failure on the part of many pastors deliberately and consciously to be alone with God.

A coffin of loneliness

A powerful plea can, therefore, be made for a cultivation of aloneness with God. No such plea, or defence, can be made for the basic, debilitating loneliness which afflicts most, if not all, men and women. Leith Samuel quotes an interviewer in a BBC television programme as claiming that: 'Most people live in a coffin of loneliness'.[1] We are certainly all aware of the emotional and psychological problems associated with it. Many pastors spend a fair amount of their time trying to counteract loneliness in the lives of those committed to their pastoral charge. This particular pastor cannot easily forget one old lady, living by herself, who admitted that, since the last pastoral visit a month before, no one had crossed her doorstep. No one knew or observed her birthday and no one addressed her by Christian name. One colleague discovered that a woman in his parish was paying a neighbour to come in and talk with her for a few minutes several times a week, such was her acute loneliness. Paul Tournier begins his book *Escape From Loneliness*[2] by telling the story of a busy secretary in Geneva who turned on the radio every evening, as the programmes ended, in order to hear the announcer say '...and so, we bid you a pleasant good night!' She believed that it was a human voice speaking to her. In describing the situation in her office, Paul Tournier says 'Never was there a word addressed to her as a person. Who she was, how she, a foreigner, had come to Geneva after many ups and downs, the sorrows that still deeply troubled her—nobody cared about these things. Her work was appreciated, and she received every courtesy, but to all intents and purposes she remained alone'. Such cases are not all that unusual.

Pastors, busy coping with the problems of others, are not immune. The pastorate can be, and often is, an extremely lonely life punctuated by periods when loneliness becomes acute.

Lonely servants

This fact should not surprise us. God's servants, in every age, have expressed their loneliness. Jeremiah, that rugged, yet sensitive soul, expressed it in words almost rebellious in tone. 'I never sat in the company of revellers, never made merry with them; I sat alone because your hand was on me and you had filled me with indignation. Why is my pain unending and my wound grievous and incurable? Will you be to me like a deceptive brook, like a spring that fails?' (Jeremiah 15:17,18). We are accustomed to think of Paul as invariably surrounded by 'fellow workers'. Yet even the apostle could write to young Timothy, 'You know that everyone in the province of Asia has deserted me, including Phygelus and Hermogenes' (2 Timothy 1:15). Who would doubt that our Lord experienced periods of intense loneliness? He called the twelve 'that they might be with him' (Mark 3:14), but these were the very people who, when the crunch came, 'then they all forsook him and fled' (Mark 14:50 AV). Volumes are written on the Cry of Dereliction, 'My God, my God, why have you forsaken me?' but, by any standard, it is the cry of a supremely lonely man enduring the ultimate isolation.

Christian leaders, or pastors, in every generation, have experienced a strange isolation tantamount to loneliness. DE Hoste succeeded Hudson Taylor as leader of the China Inland Mission, now the Overseas Missionary Fellowship. His reaction to his new responsibilities was to say, 'And now I have no one, no one but God!' [3] In experience after experience the contemporary pastor will know exactly what DE Hoste meant. The call to leadership often involves standing alone, an experience of isolation even detachment, when the heart is crying out for relationship and company.

Why should this be so? AW Tozer claimed that: 'Most of the world's great souls have been lonely. Loneliness seems to be the price a saint must pay for his saintliness.'[4] Most pastors would not claim to be 'saints' but they still are lonely beings. Why, then, do they suffer loneliness?

Much of their loneliness derives from the fact that they are, very often, messengers bearing an unpalatable message or one which challenges the foundations on which their hearers are building their lifestyles. That, certainly, goes a long way to explain the loneliness of Jeremiah and many of the prophets. The truly prophetic message, whether from the Hebrew prophet, or the contemporary preacher, is ahead of its time and cuts across the prevailing temper of its age. It asks questions the hearers would prefer not to answer and brings challenges the hearers would prefer not to face. Faithfulness to God's word is not the straightest path to acceptance and popularity. The pulpit, physically set apart from the congregation, and often above them, is a symbol of that apartness which is involved in being a messenger, certainly of love and grace, but, when necessary, of condemnation and judgment. The preacher who wishes his people to regard him as simply 'one of them' will find it difficult to be utterly faithful. Loneliness, in terms of an apartness, is the price he has to pay if he is to convey a fearless word in his preaching.

The lonely pastor

The preacher as pastor will, of necessity, be lonely. He receives confidences; he dare not share them with another soul. Problems are shared with him; they are for his ears only. He gains insights into the intimate experiences of others; they dare not be passed on. Others bring to him the tensions which tear them apart; he fails his pastoral office if he uses them as sermon illustrations. Pastoral effectiveness is directly related to a reputation for confidentiality and that entails loneliness. Far from sharing his people's problems with his colleagues, or using them to illustrate talks and sermons far from home, the pastor cannot even share many of them with his wife. The pastor, as a pastor, is a lonely man. Sometimes he will have to suffer the other leaders of his fellowship raising and discussing a pastoral problem. To a large extent his lips will be sealed if he is party to confidential information. He will be irked by the pooled ignorance of the discussion and the substitution of imagination and mere opinion for accurate knowledge, but if the other leaders do not take the hint and end the discussion, there is nothing he can say. His is a lonely silence. Fortunate is the pastor whose fellow-leaders in a church or fellowship recognise and respect that fact.

There is also the loneliness of alleged irrelevance. Henry Nouwen, in his 'Wounded Healer',[5] has a moving passage where he talks of 'the minister, who wants to touch the centre of men's lives, but finds himself on the periphery, often pleading in vain for admission. He never seems to be where the action is, where the plans are made and the strategies discussed'. He is, in fact, discovering that so many, caught up in the complex issues of life where so much is at stake, regard the pastor, and what he is trying to say, as complete irrelevances. He neither understands nor is he competent to advise or comment. A marginalized pastor is a lonely pastor.

Nouwen uses a personal illustration to stress his point. He tells of how he was, on one occasion, standing on the bridge of a Dutch ship trying to enter the port of Rotterdam through a thick fog. 'The captain, carefully listening to a radar station operator who was explaining his position between other ships, walked nervously up and down the bridge and shouted his orders to the steersman. When he suddenly stumbled over me, he blasphemed and blurted out, "Father, get out of my way."' In subtle ways, but sometimes all too open, the same dismissal is often experienced by the preacher or pastor. He is relegated to the lonely sidelines while the real issues of life are dealt with by the skilled experts. In fairness to Nouwen's captain, he changed his mind. A moment or two after dismissing his guest he said, 'Why don't you just stay around? This might be the only time I really need you.' Initial loneliness is occasionally banished when the so-called experts come to an end of themselves, admit that they are help-lessly beaten and turn to the man of God. The point, however, is still valid; the pastor, considered irrelevant, if not useless, by many in modern society, can feel painfully lonely.

A certain distancing

There is one other area of the pastor's loneliness which is worth considering though not all would agree that it is necessary. Some pastors feel that there should be no distance between them and the members of their congregation. Others feel that there should be a certain distancing even though the cost is a degree of loneliness. Sometimes that distancing can lead to a 'them and us' syndrome but that is considered unavoidable. Those who advocate such distancing express it in a disinclination to allow others to be on first name terms with them, a refusal to forge close friendships with members of the congregation or, even, an unwillingness to practise hospitality. The pastor, they insist, should be apart and that enables him to relate fairly to all and sundry with no trace of favouritism. Barbara G. Gilbert quotes Robert Kemper in suggesting 'that the preferred pastoral decorum for friendships with parishioners would seem to be "open to all and entangling alliances with none"'.[6] Such an attitude to lead-ership inevitably involves a degree of loneliness. The pastor stands alone with few, if any, friends.

So how is the pastor to cope with his experience of loneliness and all that it involves?

It is vital that he recognises its existence and, all too often, that is not easy for him.

Ordination to the Christian Ministry does not transport any person into another category of human experience. Needs, emotions, feelings remain the same. The basic dishonesty of the Christian Ministry today is that many of us have been programmed into pretending that we are different than ordinary mortals, and many members of our congregations play the game so that they can live vicariously through us. [7]

The pressure is on the pastor never to admit to himself that he is vulnerable and that he has deep emotional needs for company, affirmation and personal support. He can become so falsely obsessed with his position as pastor that he sees his loneliness as a matter for pride. He fails to see it as the debilitating thing that it really is. When the crunch comes and he suffers 'burn out', it is difficult for him to recognise his loneliness as a major contributory factor. So, a little basic honesty is called for. The pastor, despite what he likes to think and others encourage him to believe, is only human. Loneliness is a denial of his humanity based as it is on the image of a God of relationship, and such a denial will always be costly

Loneliness in other areas of pastoral ministry can be tolerated if the pastor has a good home life. John T Carson, in his biography of Frazer of Tain, [8] tells how Principal Rainy of New College, Edinburgh was, on one occasion, passing through a difficult set of circumstances. A friend remarked, 'I don't understand how you are so calm and serene'. The Principal's reply was, 'Well, you know, I'm very happy at home'. A sense of isolation or apartness can be accepted in areas of public ministry if, in the home, and among the immediate family of the pastor, there is intimacy, acceptance and love. Many a pastor has learned, sadly, sometimes when it is too late, that his loneliness is only exceeded by that of his wife, deprived of his company, as she is, at all times of the day by the demands of the congregation. His answer is to set apart quality time for his wife and family and to be disciplined in blocking out days in his diary when the family, or he and his wife, can rejoice in each other's company.

What is distressing is to note, in far too many biographies of great preachers and pastors of the past, that there is little mention of the man's wife. In diaries, or published journals, the wife seems to merit sparse notice and the suspicion lingers that she played little part in her husband's ministry. Perhaps the men would have escaped the ravages of discouragement and the belief that they were ploughing a lonely furrow if they had been more aware of their wives.

Support groups

Support groups have a valued role in dealing with pastoral loneliness.

The central value of a support group seems to be having a place where one can be honest, accepted, affirmed and supported in growing and dealing with whatever is going on in one's life. [9]

A support group is not a place where confidences can be spilled out and all pastoral restraints thrown to the winds. It is certainly a place, or more accurately, a group where a human being can be honest and open but it will also respect and honour the implications of pastoral confidentiality. To the members of the group the pastor can bring his fears and doubts, uncertainties and questions. He can, in modern parlance, 'hang loose' or be himself. He can laugh or, if he needs to, cry. Part of his loneliness is that he has been unable to do these things while being a pastor to others.

Who should be members of his support group? Some will prefer that the members be fellow pastors who can be trusted. Others will prefer to have members of the congregation. Still others will prefer a mixture with perhaps one outside, objective member. Whatever the membership there are problems. Pastors, however loud their disclaimers, do not find it easy to confess their weaknesses and vulnerability to fellow pastors. Confession of a sense of failure or inadequacy to a member of the same congregation may lead to a lowering of respect or a wrong use of the shared problem. The pastor has decisions to make. What should not be neglected is the affirmation of the need for some such group.

One antidote to loneliness which is increasingly being explored by evangelicals is the use of a Spiritual Director. Kenneth Leech describes spiritual direction in these terms: 'It is a relationship of friendship in Christ between two people by which one is enabled, through the personal encounter, to discern more clearly the will of God for one's life, and to grow in discipleship and in the life of grace'. [10] A Spiritual Director can be a friend with whom there is mutual sharing, someone who listens for the signs of the Holy Spirit moving in us, one who questions our direction, motives and decisions. In the dynamic of that relationship the understandable loneliness of pastoral leadership and ministry begins to evaporate as burdens are shared and inner thoughts exposed to loving scrutiny.

Ministers' Fraternals

The biographer of R.W. Dale, the great Congregational leader of a past generation, tells us that 'He was acutely conscious of the solitariness of ministerial life, and of its injurious effect upon spiritual health'. [11] Dale's answer was to draw up an elaborate scheme for ministers' meetings. Dale's scheme never quite worked but it remains true that the pastor who refrains from attending the local ministers' fraternal guarantees his growing sense of isolation and loneliness. He has only himself to blame and the answer is clear to see. Such fraternals can easily be criticised and, all too often, they fail to deliver what they ought to offer. Whatever their inadequacies, however, they do provide a place for pastors to meet, to realise that they are not solitary figures working in their area for the Kingdom and that others share the same priorities and aspirations. Prayer periods in such gatherings can be an immense source of mutual encouragement and support.

One final answer to loneliness needs to be mentioned. Friendships are forged by many a pastor at University or College. The pastor's spouse will bring to the marriage their own circle of friends. Such are the demands of pastoral ministry that such friendships tend to be neglected as responsibilities increase. Hospitality, or entertainment, tends to be limited by economic or time factors, to members of the congregation. That is quite understandable, but good, well-tried friendships are meanwhile falling into disrepair. It is possible to have lots of people passing through the home and not one of them be a true friend. It is possible for guests to have stimulating conversation and no real sharing to take place. The manse family should go to great lengths to maintain their old, deep and true friendships in which they can, as they have in the past, be themselves. In such honest and well-tried relationships loneliness has little room to flourish.

We must end where we began. The loneliness which appears to be part and parcel of a pastoral and preaching ministry today, with all of its negative aspects, must be balanced by another loneliness which is 'the practice of the presence of God.' The rugged and lonely souls of the Old Testament knew what it was to be alone with, and sensitive to, their God. In Gethsemane, when our Lord faced up to the loneliness of the cross, with his nearest disciples sound asleep, 'An angel from heaven appeared to him and strengthened him' (Luke 22:43). After his arrest Paul appeared alone and friendless. Yet we read: 'The following night the Lord stood near Paul and said "Take courage!..."' (Acts 23:11).

No pastor worth his salt will deny or dismiss the responsibility he has for personal spiritual fellowship and renewal, yet how many neglect it! There is little use in wallowing in self-pity over a painful experience of loneliness if what is lacking is the renewal of disciplined and regular loneliness with God. It is supremely in that loneliness that he will find the strength to be alone among those to whom he ministers.

Dryness

The confession nearly took his hearers' breath away! The Principal, with his students sitting in front of him, admitted that, years before, when he was in a pastorate early in his ministry, he came to the conclusion he had nothing left to preach on. He felt 'preached out'. He had dealt with all the major themes, preached on all the most important texts, shared all his deep convictions. He had now nothing left to say. He had a feeling of dryness. The students, with their ministries stretching in front of them, convinced that congregations were waiting with bated breath for their arrival, were amazed. How could this be?

Yet the Principal's sad confession is not uncommon, though often covered up. Many a pastor sits in his study in some desolation on a Monday morning, or even late on a Sunday night, and wonders how he can face another Sunday and the expectant faces of his congregation. He senses an emptiness. His inner being feels parched. It is not that he has committed some dire sin and feels disqualified from standing before a congregation. It is not that he has quarrelled deeply with his wife and the idea of preaching opens him to the charge of inconsistency or hypocrisy. It is not that he has few books and skimpy resources and is unable to draw on the work of others. He just feels empty with nothing worth while to say. The well has run dry.

The signs of dryness

John Updike begins his novel *The Beauty of the Lilies* by telling the story of Clarence Wilmot, the pastor of Fourth Presbyterian Church in Paterson, New Jersey. Standing in his study one evening, in the spring of 1910, he finally came to the conclusion, 'There is no God.' 'It was a ghastly moment, a silent sounding of bottomless.' What was significant is that the signs had been present, for some time, that such a conclusion was coming. So it is when we admit to ourselves that we are 'preached out.' For those who have eyes to see, the signs have been apparent for a period but, sadly, the eyes are seldom those of the preacher.

One of the signs is that we have started preaching about the Gospel and the truths of our faith instead of proclaiming them as a living message. We have been reading essays from the pulpit instead of being heralds of good news. Paul S Rees quotes AC Craig, a former Chaplain to Glasgow University, as saying. 'Very quickly, as you listen to a preacher, you begin to sense whether his words are the flowering of a life or just the frothing of a mind; whether he is a genuine traveller or only a clerk in the office of Thomas Cook and Son.' [1] It is all too easy to become a travel agency clerk talking about the glories of the faith at second hand, reciting a list of biblical facts with no suggestion that they are good news. We think we are dazzling the congregation with our explanation of the Greek words behind the English text, with our knowledge of the historical background of an Old Testament prophet or with our graphic description of the cruelties of Roman crucifixion. We are, however, beginning to show that we have nothing to say, that we have lost, or are losing, the joy of being messengers.

If we are insensitive to what is happening to us then others notice, and turn away. The story is told of an old Scotswoman who, after hearing a well-known preacher, found herself saying 'Going to hear him preach is like drawing up your chair to a fire that has gone out!' [2] Howard Williams, in *My Word*, describes the experience of Thomas Jones. He had lived many years in the heart of world politics before returning to his native Wales. His experience of listening to sermons was disappointing:

I have usually heard a sermon every Sunday since my return to Wales. Of the scores of sermons I have listened to I should say not half a dozen have given me any sense of an urgent message for the congregation....Most of the sermons were essays, lectures, talks; sometimes with a pleasant literary flavour. [3]

Danger lights are flashing if we merit these strictures!

An echo of its own

Several years ago, during a preaching trip to one of the outlying islands of Scotland, I stayed the weekend with the minister of one of the larger churches. He was longing to get away and was disenchanted with ministry in general. His congregation longed to see the last of him and were, in turn, disenchanted with his ministry. I commented on the large pile of Sunday newspapers on his study floor. He admitted that he found preaching difficult and relied on the Sunday papers, even if they were a week old, to give him something to preach on. In his *Preface to Christian Theology*, Dr. John A Mackay quotes an editorial in the American magazine *Fortune*. The writer appealed to the Christian church to speak to the world with a voice in which it would hear something more than a mere echo of its own. [4] That island pastor was speaking to his congregation with a voice which was nothing more than an echo of the world's foolishness and blindness. He had lost, or forgotten, his message and, though he kept on preaching, his words were better said by the editorials and features he drew on. Because he was failing to realise what was happening, it was only a matter of time before he resigned.

Is that not a further danger sign? Instead of turning to Scripture in our preparation we find ourselves listening to the leader writer, drawing on the political or social commentator and borrowing heavily from the latest guru to capture the cultural scene. Slowly, and sadly, our words lose the authority of God's revealed word and become an echo of what our people long to leave behind on a Sunday morning. The downward process is remorseless. Our people either tire of what we have to say, and tell us so, or we weary of what we are doing. We then have nothing more to say. We are 'preached out' and we ought to have noticed the warning signs long ago.

Passion has long been one of the hallmarks of great preaching. It is not difficult to see why. We are, after all, called to preach on the 'unsearchable riches of Christ', to tell men and women what Christ has done for them and to offer hope and forgiveness to guilty and despairing sinners. In his *The Sacrament of the Word* Donald Coggan quotes Dame Veronica Wedgwood's words: 'passion without which no major work can be written'. He goes on to say, 'We might go further and say: "passion without which no great piece of music can be performed", and "passion without which no great sermon can be preached."' [5] 'Exciting' is an overworked word in our modern language but it is difficult not to use it when you consider what true preaching is all about. It is a serious matter to 'persuade men' but it is also deeply exciting in the best sense.

When the excitement, or, rather, the passion goes then something serious is happening. We sooner or later sense that we are mouthing platitudes. We no longer feel the wonder of what we have been commissioned to communicate. Tired of eternal truth, and that is what it amounts to, we feel that we have nothing new or fresh to say. We are 'preached out' and dry within.

The necessity of review

There could well be other danger signs some, perhaps, uniquely our own. What is important is that we recognise what is happening and, before attempting to rectify the situation, we investigate the cause. What has dried us out? What have we lost? Even if we have not reached the fatal 'dried out' condition it could be profitable for every preacher to sit down, from time to time, and review his situation. 'Are there factors in my life and ministry which, if not dealt with, will harm my pulpit effectiveness?' 'Am I allowing my standards to slip and cutting too many corners?' 'Am I growing careless and slipshod in my preparation?'

It takes courage to examine ourselves in this way. Occasionally we shall have to enlist the help of a good, and candid, friend. If we are fortunate in having a support group then we can ask them to be frank with us. Wives have a role to play here. Their criticisms or comments, are seldom, if ever, meant to discourage—quite the opposite in fact, and it is a foolish man who does not listen carefully.

What are they likely to point out?

Reading habits

They may well suggest that something is wrong with our reading habits. For many of us that will prompt an immediate reaction: 'Nonsense! I keep up to date with my reading. Why, I've spent the last six months reading so-and so's latest theological offering!' Some others will take the criticism to heart. A recent investigation of the reading habits of colleagues in the ministry led to the suspicion that too many of them read no more than two or three books in a year. What they tended to read, when they did read, was the latest Christian best-seller, the sort of thing found in abundance in every Christian bookshop and demanding no great thought or concentration. CH Spurgeon, in his *Lectures To My Students*, has a fascinating chapter entitled: 'To Workers With Slender Apparatus'. He writes: 'Forgo, then, without regret, the many books which, like poor Hodge's razors, of famous memory, "are made to sell," and do sell those who buy them, as well as themselves.' Hodge has been well forgotten and best-sellers, especially those based on experience or describing the latest Christian phenomenon will follow him into forget-fulness. They should have a low priority in our study.

If we find, in our investigation, that we are only reading the theological 'heavies' then we have some further questions to ask. 'Is our reading tending to produce sermons more arid than lively?' 'Am I being a theologian in the pulpit rather than a messenger of good news?' J Oswald Sanders quotes a son's comment on his father's preaching: 'Though he spent much time and pains on his sermons, he did not cut a channel between them and his reading.' [6] That, too, is a problem which we could well identify. If we keep our reading in one compartment and our preaching in another, and never allow the two to meet, then little wonder our preaching becomes parched. Something is blocking the flow and it is no surprise that a well is running dry.

There is little excuse for sparse or neglected reading. If we put nothing into our minds then, sooner or later, nothing will come out. It is interesting, say at a year's end, to look back over the preaching of the past year. Most of us will be surprised at the sheer quantity of our output. We should not be surprised to realise that we cannot maintain that, year after year, before the same people, without an adequate reading input. Most excuses don't bear examination. The most common is that we can't afford modern books. Certainly, they are expensive but some further words of CH Spurgeon, in the chapter already mentioned, are worth quoting:

Leave mere dilutions and attenuations to those who can afford such luxuries. Don't buy thin soup; purchase the essense of meat. Get much in little. Prefer books which abound in what James Hamilton used to call "Bibline," or the essence of books. You require accurate, condensed, reliable, standard books, and should make sure that you get them.

In plain English that simply means that we should be judicious in our buying and reading. We do not need to spend huge sums of money. Impulse buying will have little place in our strategy. Instead, we shall keep an eye on reviews, if we can, or listen to well-read colleagues and buy and read only what is really saying something of value. The highest compliment the late

Andrew MacBeath, one time Principal of Glasgow's Bible Training Institute, ever paid to a book was to say that it was 'mind stretching.' Better to spend a little on such volumes than much on thin soup. Incidentally, John Wesley, whose passion for reading was mainly indulged when he was on horseback, told the younger ministers of the Wesleyan societies either to read or get out of the ministry!

Personal discipline

When we are assessing our reading habits it will not be long before we start asking questions about our personal discipline. Years ago a Glasgow sociologist suggested that the busiest men he knew were pastors and, equally, the laziest people of his acquaintance were also pastors. We all know how easy it is to get slack in essentials. No one is looking over our shoulder and we are never the subjects of a time and motion study.

Four miles before breakfast!

There is a closer relationship than we sometimes admit between our spiritual state and our physical discipline. Years ago the students in our College were all presented with a heavy volume by Nels FS Ferre the American theologian. We did not take kindly to it and it has disappeared, long since, from my study shelves. One little book by him, however, is still there and valued. In *Making Religion Real* he tells the story of a young theological student who confessed to his professor that he had lost his faith. 'You used to be an athlete in college, didn't you?' asked the professor. The young man admitted the fact. 'Get up each morning and run four miles before breakfast; then come back in three months and see me,' advised the older man. The student did as he was encouraged and his faith returned. 'It is easy to explain how you got your faith back,' said the professor. 'I saw that you had been used to running, had become flabby all of a sudden. In that state everything was bound to seem unreal to you.'[7]

That story rings a bell. I remember, on one occasion, feeling jaded and weary and wondering why. A little thought brought home the realisation that most mornings I spent sitting in my study. There was nothing intrinsically wrong with that. The afternoons were spent travelling by car between pastoral visits (again, quite commendable) but in too many of them I had a cup of tea and a bun. A rushed meal in the evening was the prelude to yet another meeting. I was a busy, faithful pastor, ignoring my body's well being and heading for spiritual exhaustion. The evidence was there in Monday morning's feelings!

A disciplined approach to our bodies will not involve, for most of us, running four miles before breakfast and for that we must be thankful! It will involve, however, a good balance between work, recreation and sleep. It will certainly involve a decent measure of exercise. Some will jog on a regular basis, others will hill-walk, others will play golf (though that can cause severe anxiety symptoms!) and some may work out in a gym. If flabby bodies lead to jaded minds and arid spirits then who knows the difference fit, well exercised and rested bodies will make to our preaching!

An outrageous scandal

We need to look at the discipline of our activities and priorities. Most of us like to be regarded as 'busy.' Before he was well known, I was given a copy of Eugene Peterson's *The Contemplative Pastor*. To him, to be called 'busy' is not a compliment:

the word 'busy' is the symptom not of commitment but of betrayal. It is not devotion but defection. The adjective 'busy' set as a modifier to 'pastor' should sound to our ears like 'adulterous' to characterise a wife or 'embezzling' to describe a banker. It is an outrageous scandal, a blasphemous affront. [9]

Strong words, indeed, but there is much truth in them. Eugene Peterson gives as one of the reasons why we are 'busy' the fact that we are lazy. 'I indolently let others decide what I will do instead of resolutely deciding for myself. I let people who do not understand the work of the pastor write the agenda for my day's work because I am too slipshod to write it for myself.' What Peterson says in that chapter should be read time after time, especially by the pastor who finds himself so overworked and drained by the demands and expectations of others that he dreads mounting his pulpit.

Lord Acton of Aldenham's words should be framed and hung on every pastor's wall: 'Mastery is acquired by resolved limitation.' That 'resolved limitation' may involve blocking off parts of the day or the month in our diaries and insisting that they are for personal reading, prayer, family relationships or recreation.

Distractions

Pastoral ministry is the target for many distractions. We begin our ministries well aware of our priorities and before we know what has happened we have accumulated all sorts of responsibilities which are, if truth be told, distractions. Some of them are very attractive and give us the feeling of usefulness but they divert us from our real work of pastoral care and preaching the Word. I once heard a colleague boast that he had three school chaplaincies, was chairman of the local Community Council, was a member of several clubs or societies and was heavily involved in several committees of the church at large. A good argument could be put up for the chaplaincies but surely someone else could have met his other commitments. His preaching, at least, with all its necessary long term preparation must have suffered. It was not surprising to discover later that he found preaching difficult and uncongenial.

Amaziah gave some advice to Amos the prophet who was a thorn in the flesh of Israel and its King Jeroboam: 'Get out, you seer! Go back to the land of Judah. Earn your bread there and do your prophesying there' (Amos 7:12). Amos refused. Many a pastor gives in. The situation is difficult in his church. Opposition is mounting to his preaching. Problems abound and support appears to be dwindling for a ministry which he believes is of God. Suddenly he hears the suggestion, akin to that of Amaziah's, that he should escape or divert into outside interests or that he should be involved in several denominational committees. He listens and begins to deprioritise (what a word!) his preaching and concentrate on these wider interests. His preaching begins to lose its edge. The resistance he found so trying declines. Life is increasingly busy but much less stressful. Preparation has to be fitted in at odd moments. Should he be surprised when, eventually, preaching becomes a problem to him? It may be that, when we find ourselves in a comparable situation, we should go back and look at the reaction of the faithful Amos and reorder our lives.

Nels Ferre tells the story of a man who had such a remarkable spiritual experience that he wrote down the account. Some time later he moved to another town and, in due course, his new pastor called to inquire into his spiritual standing. The man remembered his written account and went to recover it from the trunks stored in the basement. Returning after a long while, he stammered 'Pastor, the rats have eaten my spiritual experiences!' [9] Now, it would be easy to suggest that, when we feel dried out in the pulpit, the 'rats' have somehow got at our devotional life. A chaplain in one of our universities had a rather disturbing habit. One of his flock would pour out some personal problem to him, usually that of an unsatisfactory relationship. They would expect a clever reply but, instead they would hear him say, 'I think you have been neglecting your prayers!' So, it could well be, that, when we feel preached out, we have been neglecting our prayers. The dryness in the pulpit is simply a reflection of a dryness of heart and spirit.

Yet I doubt if the problem is as simple as that. We still pray and read our Bibles devotionally. We still have regular prayer with our spouse or the family. The real problem is that it is all hurried and we have been using the same form and pattern for years. It has all become formal and routine. We are in a rut. Prayer and scripture reading have become as exciting as washing and shaving every morning before breakfast. Our minds wander and we forget what we have read seconds after the book is closed. We feel dry, with nothing to give in the pulpit and cannot understand it for we still 'say our prayers'.

A fresh approach

We need a new method, a new approach. *Travellers' Tales* contains the findings of research undertaken by four Baptist ministers on the spirituality of colleagues, especially in relation to the demands and stresses of ministry. One quotation early in the booklet reflects the feelings of many:

In discussion with a group of Baptist ministers the feeling was that a lot of the stress and frustration we experience are (sic) rooted in our neglect of basic spiritual disciplines...'

The authors ask: 'What do ministers do when they pray?' and they go on to say:

The variety is amazing and it is important to acknowledge that we need to find our own patterns, explore. These may be different at different times of life, for to quote Carl Jung: 'We cannot live the afternoon of life according to the programme of life's morning'. [10]

Our American friends would suggest the value of keeping a devotional journal, others would stress the value of having a Spiritual Director.

A spiritual director may be a person who is trained in the art of spiritual direction, or a colleague with whom there is mutual sharing. A spiritual director or a soul friend is a person with whom one meets regularly, and who helps by listening for the signs of the Spirit moving in us. It is someone who cares for the unique unfolding of the image of God in us and who will be with us in the wilderness as well as in the faith-filled times. Many of us find that we put our spiritual growth on hold when life gets too busy. A regular time with a spiritual friend, a specific discipline, or a group focused on spiritual growth are several ways to keep this part of us alive and growing. [11]

Boredom springs from habit and saps spiritual vitality; freshness of approach has much to commend it. When dryness afflicts the approach to preaching some new pattern of spirituality could go a long way to dealing with the problem.

The fire keeps burning!

In Bunyan's *Pilgrim's Progress* there is a delightful episode in which Interpreter shows Christian a fire burning against a wall 'and one standing by it, always casting much water upon it to quench it; yet did the fire burn higher and hotter.' When Christian queried the meaning he was told that 'This fire is the work of grace that is wrought in the heart: he that casts water upon it to put it out, is the Devil.' He was then taken to the backside of the wall and saw the reasons for the fire's continual burning. 'He saw a man with a vessel of oil in his hand, of which he did also continually cast, but secretly, into the fire.' Christian is then told that the figure with the oil is Christ who 'maintains the work already begun in the heart.'

Dryness may afflict us all from time to time or, to use Bunyan's figure, the fire in our hearts and spirits burns low. Ultimately it is Christ's continuing work of grace which keeps us going and enables the fire to burn again. Ministry is a continuous discovery of the grace of God!

Failure

The organisers, and the majority of those who attended, were delighted with an evening rally during our annual assembly. Several carefully selected speakers had described the progress and growth they had experienced in their churches. The atmosphere was warm and the hint of triumphalism was in the air. Most came away feeling, with some justification, that 'the churches were in good heart.'

At least one pastor did not share the general euphoria: 'It made me feel depressed' he confessed. 'I've tried all the new ideas, and the old ones too, but nothing seems to work. I've tried to preach God's Word faithfully but there's been no response. I've failed!'

That pastor, and there are many like him, is in for a rough ride. When a vacancy committee is looking for a new pastor the denominational year book will be consulted and his static, or declining, church statistics noted. His name will be quickly placed to one side. Being an avid reader he will devour the latest best seller telling the story of some mega-church. 'Adopt my approach and you'll soon have a big church!' It only deepens his sense of personal failure. He will note the potted biography of some well-known speaker. 'Since becoming pastor of Brownville Church the membership has trebled.' He wonders what his own introduction would be. 'Since going to Whiteville the membership has decreased by 10%.'

'If you feel discouraged or a failure sing some praise songs' he'll be told. He tries. So many of them have a triumphalist note. 'You'll always be victorious and the enemy will languish at your feet', seems to be the general message. He wants to believe but the facts are inescapable. The problems seem intractable. The people appear unresponsive. The numbers are declining. Has he failed?

Our pastor is not a figment of the imagination. He exists, and dozens like him, in any gathering of ministers. Let some expert in church growth, usually from across the Atlantic, run a conference and he will attend usually because he has a deep seated desire to see the church grow, certainly not because he is a lover of the recent gimmicks. He is genuine, sincere, committed, but underneath lurks a sense of his own inadequacy and failure.

Success oriented

Part of the trouble is that we live in a society where success matters. Maria Boulding, in her remarkable little book, *Gateway to Hope*, has written:

Life in the western world today tends to be success orientated; from childhood we are exposed to influences which raise our expectations of ourselves or project on to us the expectations of others. [1]

That orientation has penetrated the church. A friend, after visiting the USA, told the story of a hurriedly called emergency staff meeting. There had been three responses to the altar call in the church along the road on Sunday morning where they had recorded none! Perhaps apocryphal, but it has more than a slight ring of truth!

Terminated pastors

There is certainly an accelerating attrition among pastors. Charles Colson in *The Body*, points out that over an eighteen month period ending early in 1989, over two thousand Southern Baptist pastors were forced out of their churches; 46% of them for failing to live up to expectations. That is, 966 of them were asked to leave because of failure to produce the results their churches expected of them. [2] The same situation is beginning to be experienced in the UK. When considering rises in ministerial stipends laymen have been heard to ask, 'Are we really getting our money's worth?' Millard Erickson comments:

there is now a tendency to regard (pastors) as employees and set performance standards which they are to meet. Rural congregations of an earlier time realised that results do not always correlate with effort....With increased urbanisation and upward mobility of congregations....management by objectives with strict expectations of performance has become the fashion. Managers who are held to strict accountability on their jobs tend to transfer such standards to their pastors, not realising that working with volunteers is quite different to working with subordinates. [3] Increasingly evangelicalism is becoming pragmatic. It does not ask so much whether ministry is doctrinally sound and in keeping with the basic theological position of the church, but what results it is producing. [4]

Pastoral care

One other area of failure is worth identifying; that of failure in pastoral care. For a pastor there is no more distressing area of failure. We can see the evidence of what we believe to be our failure in the ruined lives, broken homes and wounded spirits of the people we claim to be looking after. Neither the evidence of our failure nor the questions our failure stimulates easily disappear. Months, if not years after, we are still asking 'Could I have handled it differently? Could I have done more? How responsible am I for the present situation?' We can all agree with Stephen Pattison: 'Failure in altruism is a uniquely cruel experience.' [5]

Four questions have to be asked:

To what extent must our sense of pastoral failure be offset by the personal responsibility of those for whom we care? In every church there are those who will keep the pastor at arms' length or, even, deliberately refuse to disclose to him the problems which are eroding their spiritual or emotional wellbeing. Their motives for doing so may be varied and, sometimes, indefensible but they are nevertheless real. Often the pastor, and what he has to offer, is rejected. He is left to puzzle over his failure when, in truth, he ought to grieve over the failure of those who have rejected him.

The deacons and leaders of a church were reviewing the situation. As they looked at the past they noted that there were some within the congregation who had 'problems that were not known even to the pastor or house group leaders. We were not convinced that our intelligence network was as efficient or reliable as it could be.' What they did not do, or lacked the courage and honesty to do, was to lay the responsibility for this state of affairs, not on an 'intelligence network' easily confused with gossip, but at the door of those who refused, for whatever reason, to share their needs with pastoral carers.

It goes without saying, too, that there are some sheep intent on straying and, no matter how energetic and devoted the shepherd, they will do so. Who has failed here, the shepherd or the sheep? No doubt the shepherd will blame himself but, surely, it is the sheep who are to blame. During a long hill walk in the north of Scotland I met a shepherd with his dogs. They had spent a long, tiring day hunting for a missing ewe and her lambs on the side of the hill overlooking a sea loch. While we talked he suddenly saw the missing animals and sent his dogs to recover them. On the careful approach of his well-trained dogs the ewe, followed by her lambs, jumped into the water, swam out into the loch and all were drowned. I left the shepherd sitting on the side of the loch with his head buried in his hands and grieving. Most pastors will sympathise.

The conclusion has to be reached that, in a number of cases, in every church, the failure does not lie with the pastor despite what he may feel.

Playing at God

The second question is directed at the pastor. To what extent must his sense of pastoral failure be due to his attempt to be like God or displace him?

Everyone in a caring profession has a deep seated need to put right and mend. The desire for therapeutic power can, all too easily, develop into a desire for omnipotence that is sinful, neurotic, dangerous and verges on blasphemy. The pastor does not possess godlike powers able to solve every problem and put right every wrong. He is not God! Our greatest contribution will not be to cure and remedy every ill, but to point our people to the God who can support and strengthen them. When we attempt to be omnipotent, and feel that we should be able to answer every need, then our inevitable failure will simply witness to our sinful pride and arrogance. When we wilfully, or unconsciously, draw attention to ourselves, or cause those whom we care for to develop a dependency syndrome, then we are putting ourselves in the place of God.

If attempted omnipotence is the way to failure then so is attempted omnipresence. The Church Growth experts tell us that no one can pastor, by themselves, more than about 170 people. Many a pastor tries, usually by refusing to utilise the caring gifts of other members of the fellowship. The path to failure is to try to be involved in every crisis, present in every home, consulted in every problem and the support of everyone who struggles. Our work will become frenetic and frantic, our spirits will become burdened and eventually crushed and we shall fail. Only God is omnipresent, aware of, and involved in, every need at the same time.

The wounded healer

The third question is: To what extent is our sense of failure due to our refusal to be open about our own weaknesses and experience? Most pastors are aware of the concept of 'the wounded healer', the person who, out of their own experience of weakness, is able to reach out and help those who are bruised and hurting. The apostle Paul was such a man. 'For just as the sufferings of Christ flow over into our lives, so also through Christ our comfort overflows. If we are distressed it is for your comfort and salvation; if we are comforted, it is for your comfort...' (2 Corinthians 1:5,6). Paul was simply reproducing the experience of his Lord. 'Because he himself suffered when he was tempted, he is able to help those who are being tempted' (Hebrews 2:18).

Stephen Pattison puts it perfectly:

> Christian ministry which follows in the steps of its founder is born not from skill, power and knowledge, but from the experience of inadequacy, rejection and sorrow transformed by the love of God and then offered to others. [6]

If this is true, which we do not doubt, then the path to failure is to give the impression that we are above it all, somehow less than human, ignorant of what it means to suffer, strangers to the stresses of everyday life, unaware of the questions and doubts which plague our people. Such an impression is often conveyed by a paternalistic attitude, often interpreted as condescending and superior. Failure is guaranteed.

A false substitution

Our final question is a very practical one. To what extent is our pastoral failure due to our habitual substitution of a false kindness for the truth? The trouble with the answer to this question is that, by being kind when we should be truthful, we can delude ourselves into thinking that we are being successful pastors. There is virtue in emulating, in our dealings with those in need, the 'meekness and gentleness' of Christ (2 Corinthians 10:1). That does not mean, however, that we should be less than direct in identifying sin, disobedience and pride when we see them as the cause of the trouble. If our diagnosis is superficial, and our motivation is a desire not to offend, then our failure is certain and will come home to us, if not in time, then in eternity.

What then can be said to the pastor who has a sense of failure, either in the pulpit, in general ministry or in pastoral care?

A strict judgment

Genuine failure is a serious matter. James tells us that 'we who teach will be judged more strictly' (James 3:1). If we have been sloppy in our pulpit preparation, if we have been casual in our proclamation, if we 'have distorted the word of God' (2 Corinthians 4:2), if we have courted popularity rather than faithfulness then we are most certainly failures and we shall answer for it. If we have let people down, turned our backs on genuine cries for help, failed to appreciate the needs of our people and withheld the love which was their due from their pastor, then we are most certainly failures and responsible for it. In one of the most sobering passages of Scripture, Paul insists that 'it is required that those who have been given a trust must prove faithful.' He will not stand trial for his faithfulness before the Corinthians, neither will he pass judgment on himself even if his conscience is clear. 'It is the Lord who judges me...He will bring to light what is hidden in darkness and will expose the motives of men's hearts. At that time each will receive his praise from God' (1 Corinthians 4:2-5). Failure in faithfulness will justly fail to receive praise. There appears to be no genuine word of comfort available for real failure. All we can do is to rely on the grace of a forgiving God.

There is a huge difference between genuine, culpable failure and a sense of failure based, for example, on the absence of results or a comparison between your own ministry and that of another. To that sense of failure words of comfort and reassurance can be spoken, but they have a surprisingly hard edge.

It would be easy to say, as is often said, that we are called to be faithful, not to produce spectacular results. There is a measure of truth in that, as we shall see. What is more accurate, and sometimes harder to bear, is the fact that if we believe God has given us a ministry, then he expects us to get on with it, even though he tells us that nothing will happen. Maria Boulding puts it like this: 'Many a prophet was not merely a failure but a programmed failure. Only by failing could he do the Lord's work, yet his failure was no less painful for that.' [7]

Failed prophets

Isaiah was one such person. He responded to God's call and then was promptly told that he would fail. It was implicit in his commission. 'Make the heart of this people calloused; make their ears dull and close their eyes. Otherwise they might see with their eyes, hear with their ears, understand with their hearts, and turn and be healed' (Isaiah 6:10). It is not impossible to imagine that God sometimes sends his finest prophets into situations where the message is so challenging that there will be no response. Is that failure? It may be in the eyes of the worldly wise but not in God's.

Jeremiah faced the same situation. He knew, from the beginning, that the people of God would not listen to what he was commissioned to say. Did he feel a failure or did he not, rather, have a deep pain in his heart that the people did not hear or respond to God's word? It could be that we are called, when no response is forthcoming to our preaching, to substitute that deep seated pain for a rather self centred sense of personal failure. The failure is not ours, but that of those who treat the word of God lightly. When that happens we enter into a partnership with the Lord who cried over Jerusalem, 'O Jerusalem, Jerusalem, you who kill the prophets and stone those sent to you, how often I have longed to gather your children together, as a hen gathers her chicks under her wings, but you were not willing!' (Luke 13:34; see 19:41). Many a pastor should remember Matthew's report on our Lord's ministry in Nazareth: 'And he did not do many miracles there because of their lack of faith' (Matthew 13:58).

Of course we are called to be faithful. There is, however, no suggestion anywhere that faithfulness will lead to success and growth, though sometimes it does.

Several matters have to be looked at more closely.

The first is the assessment of success. Do we measure it by numerical growth or by a deepening spirituality which is, obviously, much more difficult to discern and will never be recorded in the official statistics? When we are talking of success or failure we do well to remember that the growth in maturity of believers does not come easily. Paul certainly did not find it easy going. 'We proclaim him, admonishing and teaching everyone with all wisdom, so that we may present everyone perfect in Christ. To this end I labour, struggling with all his energy, which so powerfully works in me' (Colossians 1:28,29).

Numerical growth?

There are even questions to be asked about numerical growth. Many of us have seen television films of American gatherings, or visited them ourselves, where great numbers gather but where the evidences of superficiality and manipulation went hand in hand with pop psychology. Was that the success we were hankering after? So before we start to feel failures we have to sit down and decide what criteria of success we are going to use. Is it numbers? Numbers can be gathered by all sorts of dubious means. I remember hearing of a theological professor who advised one of his former students that, if he wished to retain the number of young people attending, mainly young women, he should remain single! Is that an example of people responding in repentance and faith to the gospel of Christ? If that is our standard then we have to remember that we are talking of the work of the Holy Spirit. He can only do that if we are faithful. JI Packer has written: 'Leave success ratings to God and live your Christianity as a religion of faithfulness rather than as an idolatry of achievement.'

DT Niles tells the story of a Church of Scotland minister who was attending his last Kirk Session before retirement. One man had been his constant critic and he did not give up, even at the end. 'How many have been converted under your ministry?' The minister admitted that the answer was: 'Not many. In fact I know of only one boy.'[8] The boy's name was Robert Moffat who was to serve as a missionary in Africa for fifty-four years. A biographical note on this 'only one boy' says of his evangelistic work in Kuruman, Bechuanaland: 'When he left in 1870, a whole region had been Christianised and civilised, and many African Christian congregations, ministered to by trained African ministers, had been formed.'[9] There must be countless similar examples of a faithful man's apparent numerical failure being used to bring later multitudes to faith.

Goals and objectives

It is the modern habit to lay down goals and objectives. It is claimed that it is then easy to see, after a period of time, what you have achieved. Attainment is considered synonymous with success. We can, however, succeed in reaching goals we have set ourselves and still not know God's verdict on what we have been doing. The fact that I have succeeded in attaining a set of objectives, no matter how worthy, does not necessarily mean that I have achieved God's will. There is a real danger in the contemporary church of applying management standards of attainment to a sphere of activity where the real success, unmeasurable by man, is the greater glory of God.

The first conclusion we have therefore reached is that it is a dangerous, if not a foolish business, to start talking about success; either the success we have achieved or the success we have failed to experience. We can leave success, whatever it is, to God. Our responsibility is to be faithful. That is enough for any man. Our Lord warned us 'many who are first will be last, and many who are last will be first' (Matthew 19:30), and that warning is particularly relevant when we start comparing ourselves with others.

Religious clones

Russ Parker, in his little Grove Booklet entitled *Failure* has another important message for those who feel themselves failures. He writes: 'In our desire for eventfulness we all too often become a sort of religious clone trying to reproduce in our world the ministry of some other.' [10]

What Russ Parker has identified is all too common. Most pastors, especially those who have a sense of failure, would admit, perhaps privately, to feelings of jealousy and envy. They watch some master of communication at work, marvel at his 'charismatic' personality, hear his powerful illustrations and witness his growing congregations. 'If only I had what he has' finds its way into his thinking and stimulates, not admiration, but envy. We too readily forget that Paul had to deal with a similar problem at Corinth. He insists that the members of the church there were not to be clones. He uses the vivid figure of the body and insists that every member has a function and ought to perform it. 'God has arranged the parts in the body, every one of them, just as he wanted them to be. If they were all one part, where would the body be? As it is, there are many parts, but one body' (1 Corinthians 12:18-20).

There is obviously a challenge there for pastors who find themselves envying 'successful' colleagues. What is really interesting is the suggestion that God has given each one of us the gift necessary for the situation we are in, even though it is hard and unresponsive. This came home to me a number of years ago when a group of pastors were talking together. One was lamenting that his young people often deserted his church to attend a city rally addressed by someone in an itinerant ministry. They were inclined to compare their pastor's rather pedestrian approach to the scintillating, well-illustrated sermons of the itinerant. An older pastor suddenly intervened. 'That itinerant has probably only a handful of well-polished sermons with their well honed illustrations. He trots them round the country. He couldn't do what you are doing. If he had to preach to the same people, two or three times a week he would be utterly lost!' Was that cynicism or the truth? It sent that pastor, falsely made aware of his own apparent failings, back to his church with a new understanding of the value of the hard, unrelenting task God had given him and the gifts God had given him to cope. It brings to mind the comment that, after training, everyone should be appointed a bishop and, when they have proved them-selves, they should then be promoted to be a working pastor! There is no responsibility quite like it, requiring, as it does, gifts from God which the glittering itinerant does not possess.

History's greatest failure

Maria Boulding takes a strong line, using terms which verge on the dangerous: 'Jesus himself is history's greatest failure.' 'The word was made failure and died among us.' She argues that failure goes to the heart of being human and that Jesus has plumbed its very depths and redeemed it in his own flesh. This is a source of hope to all those who for whom failure seems a crushing defeat, to all those who, in fact, seek to be human and to follow the same Lord. She writes:

If you have ever been sickened by the crumbling of some enterprise into which you have put all your best effort and the love of your heart, you are caught up into the fellowship of Christ's death and resurrection, whether or not you thought of your experience in that way. God has dealt with our failure by himself becoming a failure in Jesus Christ and so healing it from the inside. That is why we can meet him in our failure: it is a sure place of finding him, since he has claimed it. So central is failure to the Easter mystery that a person who has never grappled with it could scarcely claim to be Christ's friend and follower. [11]

So, inevitably and rightly, we come to the cross. It is the same cross which Jesus asks us to take up as the badge of our spirituality. It is the same cross which Paul gloried in, even as he faced his disparaging critics. Imagine glorying in a cross, the very symbol of failure! Only as we shoulder our cross, with all the pressure to feel ourselves rank failures, can we allow ourselves to think deeply of the resurrection which lies before us. So failure is transformed.

One final word is necessary. Failure can sometimes be God's way of bringing us back to himself. In our foolishness, even as pastors, we have dreams of success, numbers, progress and development. Yet what God wants of us is not the worship of success, but trust in him, dependence upon him and obedience toward him. Could it be that he has to use the sharp instrument of failure to bring us back to being the people he can use?

Temptations

The Enemy hath a special eye upon you. You shall have his most subtle insinuations and incessant solicitations and violent assaults. As wise and learned as you are, take heed to yourselves lest he outwit you. The Devil is a greater scholar than you are and a nimbler disputant. He can transform himself into an angel of light to deceive you. He will get within you and trip you up by the heels before you are aware. He will play the juggler with you undiscerned, and cheat you of your faith and innocence, and you shall not know that you have lost them. He will make you the very instruments of your own ruin.

So wrote Richard Baxter.[1] The implication of his words is clear. Pastors are a special target for temptations launched by the devil. Some will resist such a statement and say that temptations come to all Christians, not just pastors. Surely pastors are not a special case! A moment's thought will convince that Richard Baxter had a point. Let a man be set aside to study and preach the Word, to direct sinners away from the kingdom of darkness into that of God's Son and to build up the people of God and he will be singled out by the evil one for special attention. His method will be temptation. Most pastors, often from bitter, if not hard experience, can testify to the reality of temptations directed at them through the very work they are called upon to do.

It would be easy to draw up a list frightening in its length. It would include temptations to self-pity, superiority, pride, jealousy, anger, laziness, the desire to escape and disobedience. The temptations to be patronising and to be falsely ambitious are not unknown either. The list would be endless and most pastors will confess to some familiarity with them all. What follows is not a wearisome journey through a long catalogue, but a sharing of the temptations which come to every pastor based on the temptations of our Lord.

The whole ministry of Jesus was at stake during those temptations in the wilderness. His attitudes, methods and commitment were all tested by the devil. The whole pattern of his future ministry was placed under severe examination. The description of them covers an experience of 'forty days' but the testing went on all through his ministry. So it is with us. Often there is a decisive period of temptation, or testing, when the future pattern of our ministry is determined, but the devil only departs 'for a season' and returns frequently, sometimes openly but often subtly.

Needs, gifts and worship
Jill Briscoe, in an interesting article in *Leadership* sees our Lord facing temptation in three areas; that of his legitimate needs, his spiritual gifting and his personal worship. [2] She helpfully identifies these three areas as spheres where temptation comes to every pastor. We all have, for example, legitimate needs for food, shelter and relationships. When these needs are not met, or are not met as adequately as members of our churches take for granted in their own situations, then the temptation to indulge in self pity or express resentment becomes strong.

Yet another approach identifies the three temptations to be relevant, to be spectacular and to be powerful. How many pastors, for example, would admit that they have often wished they could turn stones into bread? How relevant that would be to the hungry and deprived of the world! Yet they came to realise that man's deepest need is not bread alone 'but every word which comes from the mouth of God.' Most pastors and preachers have known the attractive pressure to concentrate on material, but ultimately superficial and inadequate, answers to human problems.

Stones into bread
The first temptation was to turn stones into bread. That is a strong temptation for the man who has the power, or ability, to do so and is hungry. As the Son of God, the Word of creation, our Lord certainly had the power to do what no mere man could do. Yet he rejected the temptation. Why? Because he was the incarnate Son of God, identifying with men and women, sharing their weakness, accepting their powerlessness and, ultimately, dying their death. He was rejecting a temptation to be superior, to avoid an essential part of being human, to use his powers to avoid a disagreeable part of his incarnation.

In a world where power often involves privilege we have been given, even as pastors, a certain position, and even power, for the sole benefit of others.

All that we have been given, even in terms of education, we could use to distance ourselves from the afflictions and suffering of our people and to protect ourselves, and our children, from what others have to endure. It is a strong temptation. We could escape and protect ourselves while making occasional forays into the world of the altogether vulnerable and needy. We have the ability to avoid an identification which will be both costly and painful, yet that identification is our calling.

Many have followed our Lord's example and refused to use their undoubted abilities in this way. The memory is strong of going to hear an old, blind citizen of Japan speaking in a London church many years ago. Kagawa was a man of undoubted ability who could have used his gifts to give himself a comfortable and good life. Instead he had immersed himself in the slums and cities of Japan and identified fully with the poor, the exploited and the deprived. Mother Teresa rejected the same temptation and shared the weakness of the poor of Calcutta.

Gordon Palmer served for a number of years as parish minister in a deprived housing estate in the east of Glasgow. He has pointed out that, too often, Christians have used their resources to move out from poorer communities such as his parish. [3] Thankfully there have been a few who, because of the call of God, have chosen to identify and move in. 'When Jesus gave the commission, do we really suppose that he meant "go where it is safe" or "Go where there is a decent class of people"? Surely his own going to the forgotten, the despised, the outcast, rules out that interpretation, but though we would never say that is what Jesus meant, that is how we take his words.' What the author did not say in the article but what is true of him, and many like him, is that though he was under pressure to live with his family comfortably outside the parish, he chose to live in it with all its noise, deprivation and discomfort. The temptation is very real to use what we have, or are, to protect ourselves when so many are vulnerable, to escape when the majority cannot do so and to be comfortable when so many we have come to help are suffering. The devil is adept at showing total identification or involvement in a bad light.

Some years ago, the situation was illustrated rather sadly late one Saturday night. A former mental patient was holed up, in a rather hysterical state, in a taxi in the middle of the town and would not leave.

Urgent attempts were made to contact her carer, who had the resources and knowledge to help. It was his weekend off and his telephone number was ex-directory. There was no way the exchange would disclose the number. Perhaps ungraciously the conclusion was reached that a good man, claiming to care for the disturbed, had succumbed, for the best of reasons, to this temptation. He was using his position to protect himself from over-involvement with the very people he claimed to help.

The Bread of Life

To reject the temptation to turn stones into bread is to reject, also, a certain superficiality of approach. People wanted, even claimed that they needed, bread. Yet, in refusing to use his power to provide all the bread they needed, our Lord was pointing to a deeper need in people's lives, that of the Bread of life.

The same temptation is not unknown in Christian circles. At the risk of being misunderstood, it has to be said that the way to be accepted, even popular, is to concentrate on meeting people's material needs to the exclusion of all else. The danger was brought powerfully home a number of years ago when a missionary was describing his involvement in relief work in Bangladesh. 'It suddenly hit me', he said, 'that, by giving all my time and energies to food distribution, I was helping to send well-fed heathens to hell!'

Certainly great sections of the population are insisting that their essential and prime needs are bread, housing, education, work and physical health. It is so easy for Christian workers to concentrate, to the exclusion of all else, on meeting these needs. Of course they can claim the mandate of Jesus who fed the hungry and cured the sick. He went further, however, and pointed to the source of eternal life and that was by taking the Bread of life. Even pastors tend to forget that and so fall to this first temptation. It is so easy to fill our days with works of social alleviation and feel that we are getting to grips with the real problem. It is so easy to challenge our people with social responsibility and soft-pedal the call to 'make disciples of all nations.' It is so easy to offer bread when we should be concentrating on the Word of life.

Throw yourself down!

In the second temptation we are told that our Lord was taken, by the devil, to the highest point of the temple. '"If you are the Son of God," he said, "throw yourself down. For it is written: "He will command his angels concerning you, and they will lift you up in their hands, so that you will not strike your foot against a stone."' (Matthew 4:6).

The Lord's trust in the Father was the target of this temptation. It is interesting to notice, almost in passing, that the devil attacked one of the great strengths of our Lord's character. The tempter does not always go for our vulnerable, weak points, rather he often attempts to corrupt our strengths. Let a man be courageous and the devil will attempt to turn it into bravado. Let a man be trusting and the attempt will be made to turn it into presumption. Gentleness will be attacked with the goal of making it weakness. High principle and deep conviction will be tempted to become inflexibility and attempts will be made to degenerate saintliness into an ugly priggishness. The pastor with great strengths of character is not immune even as our Lord was not. In a sense the devil does not need to trouble himself with our weaknesses. He already has us there. So he attempts to corrupt our strengths.

A man may have the gift of preaching and may be a means of encouragement to others. So the devil targets his preparation; suggesting that he does not need to put in so many hours of study if he has this gift. 'Why don't you just go into the pulpit and say what God has given you?' His pride is attacked. 'If you have this gift why do you stay with this small congregation; why do you accept these minor engagements? You were meant for something bigger than what you have!' Such suggestions, added to a sense that you are being taken for granted by those among whom you presently minister, can be a powerful snare in a pastor's life. Some time ago a preacher announced from the pulpit that others were right in their comments to him. He realised himself that he had a rich ministry of prayer! What he was doing, in fact, was making a public announcement that he had fallen to temptation. His prayer ministry had become a source of pride and superiority. Our strengths can be a means of entry for the devil and his temptations and, accordingly, have to be guarded with care.

Chapter 7

Trust needs no proof

Our Lord's great strength was his relationship to his Father. So the devil aimed his attack at his trust: 'You can only talk of trusting your Father if you have put his ability and faithfulness to the test!' If our Lord had jumped, as he was encouraged to do, he would have been expressing doubt in the Father's ability. It did not need to be proved. It was sufficient to trust. Trust which requires constant proof is really doubt or uncertainty.

Trust is sufficient in itself. It needs no proof, no assessment of the risk involved, no demand of a fallback position of safety if it fails. Yet most pastors, and others in Christian service, know the reality of this second temptation. We claim that we are living by faith yet we attempt to have our own safety net. We talk about trust in a faithful God, we preach about it, we challenge others with it but we like our own 'fall back'.

The poet expressed the temptation perfectly when she wrote:

Faith is a fine invention for gentlemen who see, but microscopes are prudent in an emergency.

We are tempted to make money our particular safety net. We look to the Lord for our salary or allowance and talk openly about the Lord supplying our needs. Yet we are tempted either to have, or to wish that we had, a nice little bank balance which we can fall back on if, for some reason, the Lord's supply is not forthcoming or sufficient when some emergency occurs. That nest-egg would relieve that little nagging anxiety which is always at the back of our minds even as we preach on the glories of trusting God, even for material things. The devil exploits our innate desire for security and suggests that it is not enough to trust God; we have to do something about it ourselves to bolster that trust. Most pastors and their wives can identify areas in their lives where the second temptation takes this form, or one very like it.

Self-imposed restriction

In this second temptation was the devil mocking our Lord's self-imposed restriction or sacrifice? As the Son of the Father, after all, it is inconceivable that our Lord would have actually struck his foot against a stone. That would not be true of those with whom he had come to identify. So he restricted himself and refused the suggestion.

The pastor is likewise called to sacrifice and limitation for the good of those whom he serves and for the glory of his Lord. Because of his calling he very often has to face experiences he would not normally have to endure. Difficulties, frustrations and sacrifices are everyday occurrences and humiliations are not uncommon. Pastors find themselves saying, 'I don't have to endure this!' and when they speak thus it is the voice of the devil saying 'Jump!'

Would First Century crowds have come to see, and perhaps follow, a man who could jump unharmed from a pinnacle of the temple? Modern bungee jumpers are brought up short by their elastic rope and attract only the curious. How different if the jumper, falling from an immense height, simply bounced uninjured on the ground!

If it was a temptation to do the spectacular or perform tricks as a means of attracting followers, then the devil has kept this one in his repertoire for a long time. Those who have fallen to this age-old temptation fill many of the religious slots on television, and some of the churches, on the other side of the Atlantic. It is always a temptation to go for cheap popularity, to try a few tricks or to adopt the latest gimmicks. Sometimes this temptation comes in the guise of a desire to make a name for ourselves or develop a certain enviable reputation among our people. Paul knew the danger of this temptation. Did he have it in mind when he wrote:

We have renounced secret and shameful ways; we do not use deception, nor do we distort the word of God (2 Corinthians 4:2)?

Compromise with the devil

Matthew tells us that our Lord's third temptation was to compromise with the devil. "All this I will give you," he said, "if you will bow down and worship me." Just think how attractive such a temptation could well be. Gone would be the hassle, the confrontation, the hostility which faithfulness to the truth often entails, the cost and the sacrifice. Instead, with a little compromise here, a 'dumbing down' of the truth there and a blurring of the otherwise sharp edges elsewhere, a quiet, trouble-free and popular life could be enjoyed. Certainly the cross would not be an option.

Pastors are no strangers to the temptation to compromise.

I have a friend who worked for several years in the prison service. When asked, on one occasion, for his reaction to a serious disturbance at his prison, he replied, 'Actually, I love confrontation. I just love the challenge!' By contrast there is a very powerful temptation in the Christian ministry to avoid confrontation and find peace, or relative peace, in compromise. The policy is not 'peace at any price' but it drifts perilously close to it. The people who have to be confronted are, usually, very strong and have the power to make life difficult, if not impossible, for the pastor. Silence can be golden when truthful words would shed blood, usually your own. You think twice when the person who has to be confronted is a long established leader in the congregation with a wide network of friends and relatives.

The strength of that temptation lies not in the fact that the pastor may be timid or fearful by nature. Rather it often has a direct relation to unfortunate experiences in the past or to knowledge of the disasters which have overcome colleagues. One pastor, for example, was the son of a pastor. The father, mainly because he confronted a powerful family in his church with wrongdoing, was given a harrowing time, was maligned, suffered dreadfully and, eventually, had to leave. The son, who surprisingly perhaps, followed his father into the ministry, experienced a lifelong temptation to avoid confrontation at all costs. Difficult situations would be approached sideways instead of straight on and dealing with people in the wrong, though not totally avoided, would be approached with half-heartedness. The fear of the results of confrontation was very real. Compromise was very attractive. Thankfully, the effect of his father's experience wore off and the temptations were largely overcome.

Confrontational preaching

Personal relationships are not the only sphere where confrontation is experienced. Faithful preaching can, and often should be, confrontational. Many a preacher knows the temptation, given a knowledge of those to whom his words will be almost too relevant, to tone down his words, fudge the challenge and blur the relevance. Compromise rather than confront becomes the unspoken policy. Preach a series of sermons on the prophecy of Amos, for example, when you know that there will be several business people in the congregation guilty of exploitation of their staff. The temptation to escape into platitudinous generalities will be strong. Try preaching your way through the Sermon on the Mount to a modern congregation with a fair sprinkling of the affluent, the materially minded and the worldly wise and the temptation to tone it all down will be very powerful. William Barclay repeats a story often told by Johnstone Jeffrey. It concerned two friends, one a preacher, who visited the side-shows of a fun fair and watched a knife thrower accurately miss his partner with every throw. 'That's like your preaching, Fred', said the friend to the preacher. 'It never draws blood!' [4] Yet, preaching, if it is to be faithful, has to be prepared to shed blood and the pastor, if he is to be true to his calling, has to be confrontational when it is required. The temptation to compromise has to be firmly resisted and the cost faced, and paid. When the pastor, dismissing the temptation, speaks the truth without fear or favour, he stands in a long and honourable tradition. It stretches from Nathan ('You are the man!') through Elijah, Amos and Jeremiah to our Lord. Paul was not afraid to hit hard, and in the right place, though some of his critics implied that he preferred a long and therefore safe distance, to eye ball to eye ball confrontation (2 Corinthians 10:10,11). He rejected the accusation of falling to that temptation and declined to regret the sorrow his words caused. 'I see that my letter hurt you, but only for a little while—yet now I am happy, not because you were made sorry, but because your sorrow led you to repentance' (2 Corinthians 7:8,9).

Paul highlights what is at stake. For the sake of peace we give way to the temptation to remain silent or to soft-pedal the truth. It comes from the devil and really is an invitation to shut a blind eye to his machinations and, in effect, be in league with him. People then are free to continue in their disobedience and sinful ways. Faithfulness requires that, like our Lord, we reject that temptation, face the possible personal cost, speak out and clarify the relevance of the Word. People, then, are able to see the evil of their ways and repent. No one pretends that resistance to this temptation is easy, but the end result is often the salvation of a soul and the greater glory of God.

Moving on–or out

Three photographs, all taken from roughly the same spot, have received a wide circulation. In the first Sir Winston Churchill, standing in the doorway of number 10 Downing Street, is bidding farewell to Queen Elizabeth. She has celebrated with him his imminent retirement, not just as Prime Minister, but from a long and illustrious life in British politics.

In the second Mrs Margaret Thatcher is leaving the same address and about to enter a car. She has been ousted, as Prime Minister, by members of her own party, after many years of office. There are obviously tears in her eyes.

In the third Tony Blair stands with his wife and children in the famous doorway. He has just become Prime Minister after his party has won a remarkable landslide victory in the polls. His presence symbolises change and progress in the years ahead. What the picture does not show is the departure, perhaps by another door, of the outgoing Prime Minister, John Major, to cultivate his garden and write his memoirs.

Very few would dare to compare pastors with Prime Ministers, but in their coming and going they, have at least, that in common. Many a pastor, at the end of years of service, faces farewells, gratitude and retirement. Occasionally, sadly, a pastor is asked or forced to leave. He does so, if not with publicly observed tears, then with inner regrets and occasional bitterness. Whenever a pastor leaves there will be a successor who comes, bright with promise, assuring of changes. The person he follows looks on from afar and wonders.

The absence of advice

Much has, rightly, been written on the ongoing work of the pastor. Very little has found its way into print on the crisis of leaving for whatever reason. The author's library has a lengthy shelf of material on preaching, pastoral work and the management of churches but nothing on the problems associated with severing the pastoral link either to move on or to retire. Not much shorter is the shelf on leadership in all its aspects but it, too, lacks much on the problems associated with handing on, or surrendering, responsibility. There is a fair amount of material on delegating and sharing leadership but little, if anything, on leaving it behind. Several books and pamphlets on retirement have found their way into the library. They deal mainly with money and contain nothing specifically dealing with the problems facing a pastor who, having committed himself night and day for several years to a fellowship of God's people, with their joys and sorrows, has now to distance himself and be alone with his books, his garden and, possibly, his regrets. Certainly there is nothing at all on the loss of role experienced by the pastor's wife.

The problems of leaving

So, what are the problems associated with moving on and away either to another church or to retirement?

There is a whole range of problems which have to be faced in the run up to the departure itself.

The first obvious problem is when and how to inform the church and, especially the leadership, that you intend leaving. Stories abound, some of them verging on the horrific, which illustrate how it ought not to be done. Most of them involve a measure of dishonesty, lack of integrity and just plain deceit. One colleague informed his unsuspecting congregation that he had been invited to preach in a large overseas church. He assured them that it had a pastor. What he did not tell them was that it was a pastor emeritus. He then arranged for a supply preacher to read the bombshell of his resignation to his bewildered people. Such behaviour does little to commend the dignity of the pastorate or honour the Lord who calls.

Honesty and openness

So the answer is honesty and openness. After all, do you keep secrets from those whom you love? Only if you are ashamed of something. It is highly commendable if a pastor feels that he can be free to share, at least with the others in leadership, the way his guidance is moving or the fact that he has been approached by another fellowship. There are dangers, of course, in this openness, but these dangers decrease in proportion to the measure of trust and unity which have developed over the years.

Trust and unity, these are important virtues. They are endangered within a church fellowship when the pastor has pursued a 'them and us' policy, distancing himself in a false and unbiblical way from those who are his 'fellow workers' or leaders. Usually the whole idea of a support group from within the congregation, often including other leaders, is anathema to such a man and he thus deprives himself of the very group with whom he can share his guidance in trusting unity. Such a pastor has no problem over timing. He keeps his counsel to himself and the announcement of his departure comes like a bolt from the blue. Sadly, all too often, it is welcomed.

When to tell? Pastors in mainline denominations, very often, have to follow their denominational rule book. Others are not so rigidly bound and are only required to give one month or several months' notice. Still the questions keep coming: Do I keep my decision to move to myself until I'm required to make it known or do I make it quite open? Most denominations in the UK are small enough for secrets to get out and gossip to spoil what we mean to keep to ourselves. The author was once told by a casual acquaintance that he was moving to another church when only he and his wife knew the facts. The acquaintance had a relative in the calling church who was given to letter writing and had assumed in the correspondence that call meant acceptance. Little, if anything, can be done to avoid such accidents, but they can lead to embarrassment, especially when the grapevine has short branches.

Retirement

It is slightly different when retirement looms. The congregation will know, or have guessed, the pastor's age. There seems little point in hiding the actual retirement date from, at least, the other leaders.

The deed is done. The departure date has been announced. It may be months ahead. If it is retirement it may be, as it was with the author, up to two years away. A whole new range of problems now face the pastor.

1 Kings 13 tells the story of the old prophet and the young prophet. The former is a tragic figure. Why did God not use him, sending, instead, a young man from Judah? Paul Goodliff, in recent Scripture Union notes, suggests that he 'stands as a reminder that with age and experience often

comes a worldly-wise accommodation with ease rather than a kind of steadfast spirit, epitomised by Caleb, that keeps faith sharp until the very end.' If that suggestion is true then the old prophet is the sort of pastor who, knowing that he has only a period to serve, 'marks time', lets things slip, refuses to take vital decisions and shuts his eyes to situations which demand action and firmness. 'What does it matter? I'll be gone soon' reflects this attitude at its worst. It is undoubtedly true that, near retirement, problems which once were pimples and were found challenging, appear to be mountains which the pastor would dearly avoid.

A recent article in an American journal made the point that by the time we are 55 years of age, we have achieved all that we shall ever achieve and that there will be no tremendous bursts of inspiration and insight. During the years which follow, our frustration level goes up and we need longer to recuperate after a stressful experience. What the far from encouraging author is implying is that, by the time you are nearing the age of 65, and thinking of retiring, you are a very dead duck. Any vision you have is only through thick spectacles! Caleb stands as a good Biblical denial of the author's generalisations! That Old Testament hero has had many successors and countless pastors have kept their vision clear and far sighted until the very end of their active pastorates—and beyond. Loss of vision, however, is a danger when we know we are going and when those we are leaving are talking and praying over their new vision for a future which does not involve us.

On the sidelines

No person, used to responsibility and active involvement, likes being sidelined. Yet, in a very real sense, a pastor who has announced that he is leaving faces that experience and has either to deal with it or come to terms with it. In a church committee, several months before a pastor's retirement date, plans were being discussed for future programmes which he had been largely instrumental in starting. One young man, with more enthusiasm than wisdom, suggested that the pastor's contribution to the discussion was largely irrelevant as 'you'll be going anyway'. He had the grace to apologise later but his remarks effectively showed the pastor that he was sidelined while the action developed.

Used to being aware of everything, or nearly everything, that goes on in the church the soon-to-be-gone pastor finds that meetings are taking place without him, discussions are taking place of which he knows nothing, policies are being formed without his contribution and there is an excitement in the air which has nothing to do with his ministry. Someone has said that, at the farewell to a pastor, the church should 'Look back with joy; look ahead with excitement'. After all, God is going to give them a new pastor with all that implies. Unfortunately the excitement sometimes scarcely waits till the departure of the old. Its premature presence can understandably be difficult to cope with by a pastor who has laboured faithfully.

It is certainly true that those who ought to know better can be painfully insensitive. If a church feels that matters pertaining to the vacancy, and beyond, need to be discussed before the pastor actually leaves is there any good reason why, given the nature of the pastoral bond which has existed, the pastor should not be told what is going on or even consulted? To behave otherwise is to run the risk of wounding a relationship which God has created and which, even though its practical nature changes, will still exist. Pastors do not cease loving and praying for a fellowship even though the pastoral bond has officially come to an end. In fact, departure sometimes makes the praying and loving more imperative. It is rather like seeing your family leaving the nest and setting up their own homes. The parents continue to pray and to love but they do not interfere. At least, that's the theory! It is the pastor who is moving out, but he fails if he cuts his people out of his mind. Even before he leaves he is praying for the vacancy and that God will send the right successor to a people whom he loves deeply in Christ. Perhaps many congregations should recognise this more clearly before they sideline him, however subtly it is done.

They can't manage without me!

One of the temptations every pastor encounters is the pressure to feel himself indispensable. He feels that, despite preaching on the 'priesthood of all believers', he must be involved, if not at the centre, then somewhere in everything of value. The effect of this on the congregation is dire but it is the effect on the pastor which is our immediate concern. He will not take a sabbatical for 'How will the church manage without me?' He cuts short his holiday in case there are problems in the fellowship which the other leaders cannot handle. His attitude is tantamount to Uzzah's 'steadying of the ark' which God judged so severely in King David's day (2 Samuel 6:6-11).

If this attitude lurks in his active ministry it will come to an inglorious climax when he starts to think of leaving. 'Will the church survive my going?' and 'How will they possibly cope without a pastor during the vacancy?' are bad enough but 'Can anyone else occupy my place and look after them so well?' is both rank heresy and arrogant pride. The symptoms of this attitude are all too obvious. They become apparent when a man claims that 'he will continue to keep an eye on the place', the implication being that without his attention it will go downhill. It is present when he interferes with the work he has, officially, left behind, when he criticises his replacement or when he encourages discussion on the work of the church or the ministry of his successor with the leaders of his former fellowship.

I'm off, then!

The day of departure comes. Perhaps the leaving pastor breathes a sigh of relief or, better still, offers a prayer of thanksgiving. The period, no matter how short or long, following his resignation has been difficult. There have been strains but they have been overcome. There have been insensitivities but they have been weathered. There have been previously unknown fierce temptations but they have been conquered. God's grace has been proved, once again, to be sufficient. He relaxes, however, at his peril! A new range of problems now present themselves. How is he going to break the pastoral tie? How is he going to tell these people, who are graven on his heart, that they can be grateful for the past but God is giving them a new future—and without him? How is he going to tell these folk, many of whom have shared with him their deepest secrets and most painful experiences, that, in future, they must accept another as shepherd and counsellor and not him?

The slightest trace of a belief that the church is a human institution will make the answers to these questions difficult. If our ministry is, in any way, an ego trip or built on our personality then we would be wise to absent ourselves from the farewell. Our words will ring hollow. The only answer is to see the church, even the small church of unworthy saints we are leaving, as holding a special place in the plan and purpose of the Lord of the Church. We leave it in his will and our successor comes as his choice, so Christ's glorious provision for his Church continues. We have simply played a small part in that provision by his grace and the Lord is taking his, not our, church on to a new future. To convey that with authority and conviction is to introduce to the pastoral severance a degree of anticipation which can only bring glory to God.

Even more temptations

So we leave either to a new pastorate or to read the books which have long challenged us from the shelves and tend the garden we have long dreamed of cultivating. Beware! Temptation is alive and kicking but in new and painful ways!

Some of these temptations have to do with your successor. He will, rightly, institute changes. His ministry will not be a carbon copy of yours and neither does anyone expect or want it to be. He will probably be younger and fresher. Some folk who drifted away under your ministry will begin to drift back. Some who played little part during your years will feel free to emerge and even become prominent. Programmes which were tired and struggling will suddenly have a new lease of life. The pastor's residence, practically neglected for financial reasons when it comes to redecoration or improvements, is given a glorious and expensive face lift.

The temptation is to feel that all, or nearly all, you stood for has been rejected. You feel sore that Mrs Bloggs is obviously happy under the new ministry when she manifestly rejected yours. You compare the increase in numbers with the level of attendance in your day and find yourself thinking dark thoughts. You hear the adulation and the praise and, instead of giving God the glory, you think of the way you were taken for granted and the discouragements which almost became a way of life. You begin to watch for your successor's mistakes and shortcomings and compare his decisions, unfavourably of course, with your own.

When thoughts like these begin to grip you then you are in deep, deep trouble! It is no consolation to realise that they are common to most pastors who have moved on. Such thoughts are wrong; they have to be repented of and dealt with before the Lord of the Church. Selfishness, self pity and pride have been enjoying a field day when they should have been firmly rejected. The church is Jesus Christ's, not ours, and he has instituted a new chapter in the life of the fellowship we served. We may not see it clearly, in our foolishness, but the new ministry is probably building on the foundation which we were privileged to lay down. Our bruised ego is blinding us to the essential continuity of God's workings. The methods, plans, even the materials are different, however, and rightly so. The church has passed to a new stage in its life where a different approach is needed, a new voice will be helpful. All that is as it should be. Joshua had a role and a ministry altogether different from that of Moses, but we do not compare them in order to dismiss one at the expense of the other. Each was God's man for the time in which he lived, and times change.

Our attitude, if we have moved physically far away, should be that of thanksgiving that the God of 'new things' is doing just that, where we were slowly falling into a tired rut. If we are geographically near, then we can engage in the ministry of encouragement. Warren Wiersbe, in a recent magazine article, puts it bluntly: 'Get out of the way of your successor and try to be an encouragement…Treat him the way you want your predecessor to treat you when you arrive at your new field…If you return treat him as your pastor.'

Out to grass?

Retired pastors have to struggle with the thought of being discarded and being put out to grass. They are encouraged, in this, by the culture of the western world. When you reach a certain age you are finished, you have made your contribution. You have to get out of the way and allow a young person, often much younger, to take over. So much is happening and you are no longer part of it. When the denomination looks for someone to fill a certain responsibility you are understandably not considered. When you go as preaching supply to a strange church you overhear some bright youngster say 'It's some old retired minister this morning!'

New problems and changing cultures demand fresher minds and you are often made to feel old fashioned, incapable of coping with change and inflexible in your attitudes. You are regarded as having yesterday's answers to today's problems and that may well be true. The bewildering array of moral, social and ethical problems which face society today leave you confused and expose the fact that developments have left you behind. Your old and faded College notes do not deal with In Vitro Fertilisation, surrogate motherhood, co-habitation and living wills.

What do you do? You can give in gracefully and admit that you are rapidly out of touch, that your mind has grown tired and content yourself with *Coronation Street* or *Neighbours*. On the other hand you can now read all the clever books that the youngsters confess that they have no time to read. You have the leisure now, if you have retired and still practise self-discipline, to grapple with some of the larger commentaries and wrestle with some of the massive tomes which mocked you from your shelves when you were 'working'. A fresh mind can often exist in an older body!

A silent telephone!

Undoubtedly, if we are facing retirement, our lifestyle and general pattern of life will change drastically. Deadlines will be largely things of the past. Church committees will cease to fill our evenings. Diary pages will even be blank! The telephone will no longer go incessantly—usually just when we were sitting down to a meal. The pension will replace the monthly salary and that could well bring its own trauma! We shall find ourselves sitting in a congregation more often than standing in a pulpit. That could well be salutary. If we had known how uncomfortable these pews were we would have cut the length of our sermons! Why didn't someone tell us?—or, weren't we listening when they did? We spent our whole ministerial life insisting that status and position were unimportant only to discover, when we retired, that we have lost our undoubted status and position and, occasionally, it hurts. Perhaps the virtue we need most is contentment and it is no accident that it goes hand in hand with godliness.

Looking back, from a new pastorate or from retirement, is inevitable. The mistakes loom large through the mists of receding time. The questions crowd in and threaten depression and doubt. Should I have done this instead of that? Could I have managed difficult situations better? Was I too hard with so-and-so and too soft with someone else? Did my preaching miss the mark too often? Wordsworth thought of daffodils when lying on his vacant couch but to the reminiscing pastor, in his lonely moments, failings and doubt flood his troubled mind. Such thoughts are understandable if we believe that we shall give account of our stewardship. We shall account for the 'wood, hay, straw' we used and the 'gold, silver, precious stones' which we sometimes neglected as we built. The bottom line is that the Lord uses 'vessels of clay' and with him there is abundant forgiveness.

Every problem, and there are many, connected with moving on or retiring, has to be dealt with, as we have seen. Ultimately the answer is to realise that the church belongs to Christ, her Lord, and can be safely left in his keeping. He brought us to that band of people and he is now moving us on. He will look after their future and has a purpose for them greater than our worries. We, too, enter a new chapter in our lives and ministry and our future lies with him.

The minister's wife and retirement

Before retirement life was so busy. The days were full, and a free evening, especially with my husband, was very unusual. The telephone rang, people were frequently coming for meals, preparation for quickly approaching meetings had to be made and these meetings attended. I was always behind with housework and ironing. There was always a book or knitting that I longed to finish. Life was a hive of activity and, looking back, I now see that I thrived on it!

I must confess that for the last few years I was tiring. I knew that I was not functioning so well and longed just to be one of a congregation rather than the 'minister's wife.' I looked forward to retirement as I had looked forward to our holidays in the past. It would be a break.

Retirement came. It was a break. The telephone was quiet, guests were infrequent, deadlines had gone, we had time for each other and to walk, read or whatever.

The big difference was that the break went on and on and I was ready to get back! Mostly I wanted to be back in my church with my folk. As the reality of retirement dawned on me I felt deeply bereaved and, at times, panic-stricken. Not only did I miss people, I missed our precious building. No longer was I 'in the middle' of lives and situations. The pattern of my days and weeks had gone and I missed the buzz of my busy days.

One of my biggest problems was a sort of paranoia. I knew in my head that it was important to detach from the congregation we had served for twenty-five years. I knew that the gap we had left would quickly close but I found myself thinking: 'Were these folk my real friends or were they friends only because I was the minister's wife?' Did I really matter to any of them? There was the gradual realisation that keeping in touch with some meant that I was the person making the effort. That prompted grief and the loss of desire to make contact. Were those who still contacted me doing it from duty rather than friendship? It took a long time to realise that true friendships have survived, but very few.

Five years on, it is easier to be detached and sort things out. I can thank God sincerely for all the wonderful people I worked with closely and happily over the years. I was privileged to be part of many a good team, but the joy of that fellowship cannot continue into my present life. I have to, with God's help, find that level of fellowship and joy in new relationships and new areas of service. At this age and stage in life that is not easy. I have to remind myself that I was often tired and weary with my hectic lifestyle, so that I can give thanks for the space and time I can now enjoy.

The most important fact I have realised is that, before retirement, my spirituality was so tied up with my activity. When that activity ceased, I floundered. The props and sparks had gone and I had to look for God in my life in new ways. As I have taken all these bereavements and disappointments to him, I have been aware of his gentle, healing hand, bringing me new joys and satisfactions. It has taken a long time to realise that the end of our ministry was, in fact, the beginning and we are still learning about this new chapter in our life.

Notes

Chapter 1 notes

1   **Tidball, DJ,** *Skilful Shepherds,* IVP, 1986, p.14.
2   **Tidball, DJ,** *Skilful Shepherds,* IVP, 1986, p.14.
3   **Temple, W,** *Readings in John's Gospel* (First Series), Macmillan, 1939, p.167.
4   **Trollope, A,** *Barchester Towers,* Pan, 1980, p.66.
5   **Trueblood, E,** *The Incendiary Fellowship,* Harper & Row, 1967, p.43.
6   The above three paragraphs summarise the author's Presidential Address to the Baptist Union of Scotland Assembly in 1971 entitled *The Ministry—or—the Abolition of the Laity.*
7   **Greeves, F,** *Theology and the Cure of Souls,* Epworth Press, 1960, p.24.
8   **Wright, F,** *The Pastoral Nature of the Ministry,* SCM, 1980, p.8.
9   **Wright, F,** *The Pastoral Nature of the Ministry,* SCM, 1980, p.25.
10   **Coggan, D,** *Convictions,* Hodder & Stoughton, 1975, p.257.
11   Quoted in **Packer, JI,** *Keep In Step With the Spirit,* IVP, 1984, p.99.
12   Quoted in **Packer, J I,** *Keep In Step With the Spirit,* IVP, 1984, p.155.
13   **Augustine,** *Sermon* CCIX.
14   **Baxter, R,** *The Reformed Pastor,* Nisbet, p.119ff.

Chapter 2 notes

1   **Middlebrook, JB,** *William Carey,* Carey Kingsgate, 1961, p.56.
2   **Peterson,E,** *A Long Obedience In The Same Direction,* Marshall-Pickering, 1989, p.12,13.
3   **Ford, L,** *The Christian Persuader,* Hodder & Stoughton, 1967, p.37.
4   **Peterson, E,** *Under the Predictable Plant,* Eerdmans, 1992, p.21.
5   **Middlebrook, JB,** *William Carey,* Carey Kingsgate, 1961, p.56,57.
6   **Robinson, JAT,** *The Difference In Being a Christian Today,* Collins, 1972, p.70.

Chapter 4 notes

1   **Samuel, L,** *There Is An Answer,* Victory Press, 1966, p.31.
2   **Tournier, P,** *Escape From Loneliness,* SCM, 1948, p.13.
3   Quoted by **Sanders, JO,** *Spiritual Leadership,* Marshall, Morgan & Scott, 1967, p.107.
4   Quoted by **Sanders, JO,** *Spiritual Leadership,* Marshall, Morgan & Scott, 1967, p.108.
5   **Nouwen, H,** *The Wounded Healer,* Image Books, 1979, p.86.
6   **Gilbert, BG,** *Who Ministers To Ministers?,* Alban Institute, 1987, p.52.

7   Quoted in *Fraternal*, Vol.229, January,1990.

8   **Carson, JT,** *Frazer of Tain*, Scottish Evangelistic Council, 1966, p.113.

9   **Gilbert, BG,** *Who Ministers To Ministers?* Alban Institute, 1987, p.59.

10   **Leech, K,** *Spirituality and Pastoral Care*, Sheldon Press, 1986, p.48.

11   **Dale, AWW,** *Life of RW Dale of Birmingham,* Hodder & Stoughton, 1902, p.204.

Chapter 5 notes

1   Quoted in *Christianity Today*, September 14th., 1962.

2   **Walker, A,** *The Whole Gospel for the Whole World*, Marshall, Morgan & Scott, 1958, p.114.

3   **Williams, H,** *My Word*, SCM, 1973, p.32.

4   Quoted by **Wood, AS**, *Heralds of the Gospel,* Marshall, Morgan & Scott,1963, p.14.

5   **Coggan, D,** *The Sacrament of the Word*, Collins, 1987, p.86.

6   **Sanders, JO,** *Spiritual Leadership*, Marshall, Morgan & Scott, 1967, p.103.

7   **Ferre,NFS,** *Making Religion Real*, Collins, 1969, p.38.

8   **Peterson, E H,** *The Contemplative Pastor,* Word, 1989, p.27.

9   **Peterson, EH,** *The Contemplative Pastor*, Word, 1989, p.77.

10   **Green, B, Jarman, M, Rackley, J, Vendy, B,** *Travellers' Tales. An exploration of resources for ministers*, 1995, p.7.

11   **Gilbert, BG,** *Who Ministers To Ministers?*, Alban Institute1987, p.62.

Chapter 6 notes

1   **Boulding, M,** *Gateway To Hope*, Collins, 1985, p.9.

2   **Colson,C,** *The Body,* Word, 1992, p.128.

3   **Erickson, M,***Evangelical Mind and Heart*, p.178.

4   **Erickson, M,** *Evangelical Mind and Heart*, p.197.

5   **Pattison,S,** *A Critique of Pastoral Care*, SCM, 1988, p.153.

6   **Pattison,S,** *A Critique of Pastoral Care*, SCM, 1988, p.152.

7   **Pattison, S,** *A Critique of Pastoral Care*, SCM, 1988, p.37.

8   **Niles, DT,** *Preaching the Doctrine of the Resurrection*, Lutterworth, 1957, p.30.

9   Article, *Robert Moffat, The New International Dictionary of the Christian Church*, Paternoster, 1974, p.668.

10   **Parker, R,** *Failure,* Grove, 1987, p.9.

11   **Parker,R,** *Failure*, Grove, 1987, p.9.

Notes

Chapter 7 notes

1   **Baxter,R,** *The Reformed Pastor,* Nisbet, 1850, p.85.
2   **Leadership,** Volume XV., No.4, 1994.
3   **Palmer, G,** *Scottish Bulletin of Evangelical Theology,* Volume 10, No.1, 1992.
4   **Barclay ,W,** *Fishers of Men*, Epworth, 1966, p.109.

Horizons of hope
Reality in disability

Brian Edwards

248 pages   £7.99

Dealing frankly with the subject of disability, *Horizons of hope* chronicles the stories of a number of Christians who have lived through the reality of personal crisis, and have a testimony of faith to share. In these pages, there are many accounts of courage, including the story of Brian and Barbara Edwards whose devotion and service despite Barbara's crippling disability were an inspiration to many. Among others, there are testimonies from the parents of a child with a chronic skin disorder, and a young lady who copes daily with the realities of Cystic Fibrosis. The book is moving for both its honesty, and the fact that through their difficulties, all concerned can see that there is a plan in their lives. *Horizons of hope* is an unsentimental, candid admission that Christians struggle and can even experience despair despite their trust in God's sovereign plan. A moving, yet thoroughly practical book which should serve as an encouragement to many.

REFERENCE: HOR
ISBN 1 903087 02 3

"A book of hope and inspiration"

Joni Eareckson Tada

Improving your
Quiet Time

Simon Robinson

144 pages   £6.95

Simon Robinson's *Improving your Quiet Time* is full of practical advice which should encourage many who are struggling to achieve a better balance in their spiritual walk. It also contains ideas for personal study plans, together with a two year Bible reading plan.

REFERENCE: QT
ISBN 0 902548 89-1

John MacArthur

"This compact book gives spiritual guidance on so many areas of a Christian's relationship with God. A delightful, practical how-to guide. Invaluable."

John MacArthur

Also from Day One

Falling short?

Chris Hand

104 pages   £4.50

With its well designed materials, and ready-to-use format, many churches throughout the UK have taken up the *Alpha Course* enthusiastically. Many others are considering whether they could use it to boost their evangelism by making the most of its apparent runaway success. But are we hearing the full story? Chris Hand has carefully observed the development of the *Alpha Course* over several years and offers an overview of its aims and methods, and asks whether it provides an authentic full presentation of the Gospel.

REFERENCE: ALPHA
ISBN 0 902548 88 3

"A quality-critique, expertly drawing together background, content, and results"

Dr Peter Masters

The Great Exchange: Justification by faith alone in the light of recent thought

Philip Eveson

Andrew Anderson, Series Editor

228 pages   £7.99

"At a stroke, Philip Eveson puts the modern reader in possession of all the facts of the current dispute about the meaning of justification, and equips him or her to take part in the debate."
Evangelical Action, Australia.

REFERENCE: TGE
ISBN 0 902548 86 7

"This piece of clear, warm theology is a priceless guide and example. Absorb, teach, rejoice in these pages! Very highly recommended"

The Banner of Truth Magazine

Churches in trouble? Developing good relationships in your church

Paul E. Brown

Andrew Anderson, Series Editor

200 pages £7.99

From New Testament times onward, churches have experienced the pain and devastation of broken relationships and disunity; sometimes among leaders, sometimes between leaders and members, sometimes among members—and sometimes between them all together! From a biblical perspective, this book is written out of deep concern to promote the welfare and harmony within churches by examining leadership and relationships issues. Published in association with FIEC.

REFERENCE. CIT
ISBN 0 902548 92 1

"This book contains a wealth of helpful material with pertinent observations and practical suggestions. There is no doubt that it will prove most useful in these confused and troubled times"

The Banner of Truth Magazine

365 days with Spurgeon

A unique, daily Bible devotional containing powerful insights from CH Spurgeon's Park Street Pulpit

384 pages
A5 Paperback £9.99
A5 Hardback £11.99

If your daily reading notes have become rather over familiar and tired, and you are looking for something more challenging, this excellent volume may really help. Here, from the archive of the young Charles Haddon Spurgeon's Park Street sermons (long before his well-known days at London's more famous Metropolitan Tabernacle) we have pearls of Biblical wisdom indeed.

What is particularly striking when reading these extracts is how incredibly appropriate they are to the ears of the modern Christian in need of genuine spiritual understanding.

365 days with Spurgeon is available in either Hardback or Paperback versions. Both have sewn binding and will offer years of service. An ideal gift.

ISBN 0 902548 83 2 PAPERBACK
ISBN 0 902548 84 0 HARDBACK

"I recommend this without hesitation—especially for short-time meditation with the family"

English Churchman

Also from Day One

Depression: a rescue plan

Jim Winter

Paperback
152 pages   £6.99

It is a staggering fact that according to the World Health Organisation, 100 million people are depressed at any one time. During the decade before the close of the millennium, the number of people in the United Kingdom consulting their doctors complaining of depression more than doubled. Little wonder that Winston Churchill referred to it as his 'black dog', and Samuel Johnson called it, 'this vile melancholy'.

The word 'depression' is used to describe a wide range of emotions and conditions ranging from momentary unhappiness to suicidal despair. To complicate matters, its cause and effect encompass every area of our being. The fact that it is so common place means that sufferers need not feel ashamed.

The Christian—despite having a living relationship with God in Jesus Christ, and the glorious anticipation of heaven—is not immune from depression! The lives of some of God's greatest servants clearly demonstrate that! This practical guide is the result of the author's twenty years experience as a clinical practitioner, and local church pastor. Without medical jargon, it offers a step by step guide to coping.

Reference: DEP
ISBN 1 903087 03 1
Publication: May 2000

The Resurrection: The unopened gift

Gerard Chrispin

128 pages   £5.99

The author believes that many Christians—while acknowledging the significance of the Resurrection—are failing to make full use of its great riches in their daily lives. The unopened gift challenges Christians to stop "sitting on the resurrection" by living in the light of the risen Christ.

Gerard Chrispin's deep concern to apply God's word in today's world is evident in this book. Its examination of the resurrection is faithful to scripture and thoroughly practical. It fills a real gap in contemporary Christian literature.

REFERENCE: RES
ISBN 0 902548 91 3

"Challenges us to live for the risen Christ"

Roger Carswell, Evangelist